To young women everywhere who are questioning their sexuality

Acknowledgements

Thanks to all our contributors, including everyone who completed the questionnaire, and their friends, girlfriends and families who supported them. Special thanks to all at Diva Books/Millivres Prowler Group, including Gillian Rodgerson, Kim Watson, Debra Doherty, commissioning editor Helen Sandler, as well as Gina Roberts, who produced most of the illustrations and contributed to the book design, on work experience.

The commitment of youth workers across the country has helped young women questioning their sexuality to write about their lives for this book. In particular, we'd like to thank Mo Hand at Freedom Youth without whose help and encouragement the residential writing weekend would not have happened; Becca Luger, the writing tutor; and The Warren, Not the Only Fruit, GLYSS and BLAGY youth groups. Special thanks go to Kerry Broadhead and Julia Tipton for their creative work with young women questioning their sexuality and to all the workers at Soft Touch Arts. Thanks also to Carola Towle at Unison, Jocelyn Watson at LAGER, Jenny Roberts of Libertas! women's bookshop, Gay's The Word bookshop, Avtar Brah, Moira Walker, Rajni Kumrai and Madinah Usman and to the many other people and organisations whose contributions, information and contacts have enriched this book.

Girl 2 Girl Edited by Norrina Rashid & Jane Hoy   First published 2000 by Diva Books, an imprint of Millivres Ltd, part of the Millivres Prowler Group, 116-134 Bayham Street, London NW1 OBA. World Copyright © 2000 Norrina Rashid & Jane Hoy who have asserted the right to be identified as the editors of this work in accordance with the Copyright, Designs and Patents Act 1988. A CIP catalogue record for this book is available from the British Library

ISBN 1 87374145 6

Distributed in Europe by Central Books, 99 Wallis Rd, London E9 5LN. Distributed in North America by Consortium Book Sales and Distribution, 145 West Gate Drive, Saint Paul, MN 55114-1065 USA, Telephone: 651 221 9035/ 800 283 3572
Distributed in Australia by Bulldog Books, PO Box 700, Beaconsfield, NSW 2014. The mention or appearance or likeness of any person or organisation in Girl 2 Girl is not to be taken as any indication of sexual, social or political orientation of such persons or organisations.

Contents

girl 2 girl

Edited by Norrina Rashid & Jane Hoy

with illustrations by Gina Roberts

How this book began

One day in the last year of the 20th century, 16-year-old Amy wasn't feeling too good about her life. After a lot of thought she plucked up the courage to tell her mother, Sharon, that she thought she might be gay. Now Sharon, although an open-minded and supportive sort of mother, is straight and felt a bit out of her depth. But she wanted to help Amy, so she went to talk to her friend and colleague Jane who was a lesbian. Her opening words were: "Jane, I have something to tell you." Jane could hardly keep a straight face as she heard this classic line. Was Sharon about to come out to her?

When the situation was cleared up, Jane took Sharon off to Gay's the Word bookshop near where they worked in Bloomsbury, London. They searched for books which might interest a young woman who was questioning her sexuality. There seemed to be very little for lesbian or bisexual girls, especially anyone living in Britain.

That evening Jane told her partner Helen about Amy, Sharon and the lack of books for young lesbians. Helen was the commissioning editor of Diva Books and she thought something for lesbian and bisexual young women would be wonderful as the first non-fiction book in the series. So did the publishers. Jane and Helen contacted Norrina, a youth worker they'd met in Bradford through a friend, and she agreed to be co-editor with Jane.

So, thanks to Amy, that's the story of how this book began. You can read one of Amy's poems later in the book.

About this book

✱ Norrina Rashid and Jane Hoy

This book is for all young women. If you are exploring your sexuality, you will find experiences which may help you understand yourself. Maybe it will answer some of the questions you lie awake asking yourself and help you find ways to cope.

If you identify as heterosexual, read on. It will show you that it is difficult for other girls growing up and questioning their sexuality, especially if their mates are making homophobic remarks and laughing at anyone who thinks just that little bit differently. We are all human and there is nothing to fear. You cannot be 'turned into' a gay person.

You might even recognise yourself as one of the young people at school who makes life unbearable. Read the book. Stop and think how you can make life more bearable for each other.

✱ Who's in the book?

The girls who wrote this book come from Wales, Scotland, Northern Ireland and England. They live in suburban towns, small villages and inner cities. They are black, white, of differing abilities; they are rich and they are poor. Some have used their real names but most have chosen other names because they're worried about negative reactions from their families and friends.

At the heart of the book are stories and poems produced by young women aged 15-21 at a residential creative writing weekend facilitated by Norrina and assisted by Becca Luger, herself a young lesbian and writer. You can read about what Fran, Sara, Lucy, Carla, Emma, Lorraine and Lee (not their real names) did in 'The Weekend' by Emma, overleaf. The weekend was sponsored by *Diva* and individuals were sponsored by their youth groups. These young women had stories they wanted to tell, but many of them weren't confident about writing them down till they took part in the workshops.

We sent interactive questionnaires to lesbian, gay and bisexual youth groups and received many individual replies. GLYSS, The Warren and Not the Only Fruit each responded as a group, working on ideas when they met each week.

We are also pleased to be able to include original artwork from First Out lesbian, gay and bisexual youth group working with Soft Touch Arts in Leicester.

College and university lesbian and gay societies were circulated and others responded through adverts in *Diva* magazine, gay newsletters, websites and the grapevine.

* *What's in the book?*

To help you find your way through the book there are six main parts. Each contains stories, poems and illustrations and sound advice on how to handle the everyday realities of life.

Sections overlap because our lives don't divide up neatly. First, 'Dreams and dilemmas' explores the hopes and fears young women face, feelings about their sexuality and controversial views on bisexuality. 'Who do you think you are?' looks at what to call yourself and how to come to terms with yourself amid prejudice and negative images of lesbians. Do you want to be called lesbian or bi or would you rather not be defined by who you fancy? One contributor, Andrew, realised that a lesbian identity didn't fit – he's a transgendered young man. Others are managing to reconcile religion and sexuality – like Julia, Naz and Salima.

'Friends and family' is about the support available from youth groups and, sometimes, from the family. With the smallest of resources, youth workers do an amazing job. Time after time, young women like Alis or Heather who were lucky enough to find a youth group tell of how it was a lifesaver.

'Out in the world' includes stories of coming out to families, friends, but firstly, yourself. Several young women came out to gay boy friends. Some young women were surprised at how much support and warmth they found when they came out. Often mums, friends, teachers and youth workers had already guessed. Other girls are still waiting for the right moment or, like Sam, regret not telling an elderly relative. There are poems about bullying with a very clear message to schools and colleges to fight for the abolition of Section 28 of the Local Government Act, which often prevents young lesbian and gay people getting the support they need.

In 'Living the life' we hear how Sarah used the internet and got more than she bargained for. Laura came out to wonderful acclaim from the whole school but got badly hurt the day after. It is a struggle, but the young women find their paths in life. And the final section from our contributors speaks for itself. The excitement, fun, longing and pain of 'Love, lust and loss'.

Other information such as contact numbers, helplines, new words, and some books and films (including the contributors' favourites) are all at the end of the book in the 'Info zone'. Finally, the editors describe their experiences working with teenagers and adults who have been affected by homophobia.

Several contributors told us how they found writing for the book therapeutic and energising; it gave them a whole new perspective on their lives. We hope reading it will do the same for you.

The weekend

Emma didn't know what to expect when she set off on a writing weekend for girl2girl...

I ripped up my bedroom looking for the right clothes. After all, I was going to spend the weekend with ten lesbians I barely knew. It made me feel that little bit anxious. What was I to take? It looked like a tornado had hit my bedroom. What the hell, it had to be done. I packed a bit of this and a bit of that. Enough clothes crammed into my rucksack for a lifetime of writing weekends.

I'd only met this Norrina character for an hour or so. She'd come over to Queens Court to talk to me about a book she was doing. *Girl2girl*, a book for young lesbians and bi girls. The idea was for young women to share their experiences and write about them. Why not? How often does a girl get to spend the weekend with ten lesbians talking about their lives and loves?

The meeting point was to be the station, my first encounter with some of the gals. The fun and jokes of spending the weekend with ten lesbians faded into the background. There was a hint of apprehension in the air. I'm expected to open up to strangers? Oh my God! What if they hate me, make fun of me, laugh at my experiences, think I'm screwed up? What if they are really cool gals with brilliant writing talents!

Norrina, our group leader, arrived. "I'm not a leader, I'm a facilitator," she kept saying. "You're going to write. I'm going to help." She played around with us, relaxed us. She had a way about her that I liked, that made me feel comfortable and relaxed. We chatted a bit on the train. Norrina wasn't there to work her magic. She sat somewhere else, listening to her Walkman. She told us she was listening to *Teach Yourself Spanish*. Ha ha.

The view outside slowly went from polluted red and grey boxes to small, cute whitewashed houses. Er, em, I think it's called the countryside! The train pulled into the station and there we were in Abergavenny. We walked towards the minibus which was to take us into the heart of the wilderness, the Brecon Beacons, deep in South Wales.

When we got closer to the bus I could see more girls hanging about. Thought we were meeting them there? But no, more new people. I felt the northern posse physically move closer together, creating an impression of an impenetrable group. The usual pleasantries were exchanged, then we crammed into the minibus packed full of baggage and jammed with emotions. Fingers drumming, arms and legs crossed, the rest a herd of nervous shuffling feet.

Half an hour later we arrived and had a tour of the gorgeous farmhouse, set in wonderful Welsh hills. Not a road in sight. And then the fight for the best bed in the house! After the big scrap, the work began…

Introduce yourself. Dance, draw, talk. Excuse me but I thought this was a writing weekend? "Wait and see, trust me," Norrina would say. It was good. We drew pictures, massive pictures about ourselves. Where we lived, best friends, where we hang out, how we chill, fave song, hottest babes. Anything you wanted really. When looking at everyone else's drawings you notice each person's favourite aspect of themselves, best clothes/accessories are over-exaggerated. I realise with my own drawing that my 'para' boots are bigger than my arms and legs put together! What will Norrina read into this? It was like a drinking session without the alcohol to use as a smokescreen over what you said. It was amazing – we shared a lot of stuff, and that was in the first three hours.

Food time! The food was gorgeous. It's not often I ask for more vegetables. But there's a first time for everything. Maybe the country air was poisoning my brain cells and killing my chocolate addiction! Thanks Mo, top chef.

If anyone has skimpy nightclothes, they have to check for ghosts and madmen wandering around. It's the rules. It's in all the films we've ever seen. We sat there in the front room, the conversations drifting from girlfriends to family to music and then back to who would be the first one murdered if a madman did break in. Can't quite see how we got there but we enjoyed the fear of it!

Morning arrived, opening up… honesty… emotions… Writing for me is an emotional thing and very personal, especially when reading out stuff that is to do with your feelings. We were all laying our shit on the floor, spilling our guts and sharing our experiences. Good and bad, it was all there.

We were dancing, drawing, making sculpts with each other's bodies. There were discussions about politics, bigots and homophobes. We did it all really. It was strange at first but I guess it got us all thinking, talking and writing.

I know it sounds tacky, but it helps listening to other people's experiences. You realise you are not alone, that other people are there or have been there and that it will be all right. I guess that's what the book is for.

Emma Hunter, 18, Yorkshire

Opposite page: photo by Geoff Manasse/GAZE   This page: photo by Laurence Jaugey-Paget/GAZE

girl2girl

Dreams and dilemmas

tell all!

I'd like to own my own private practice as a psychotherapist in Soho, London. I would have a large apartment with a huge bedroom with a four-poster bed right in the middle. My next-door neighbours would be Jennifer Lopez and Anna Ryder Richardson (I wish). I'd like a steady girlfriend who would live with me and every wall in the house would be made of those fab glass bricks. My food cupboards would be full of Battenburg cake which would just regrow when you ate it. All my clothing would be French Connection and would have FCUK splashed all over it. The car in my driveway would be a white Peugot 306 or a black Range Rover.

Becoming an aeronautical engineer and working for someone like Rolls Royce or NASA. In 10 years I want to be doing engineering work in the third world.

In ten years I hope to be in a job, like TV production, hopefully living in either London or New York. I'd like a nice flat, a dog and a girlfriend [really in that order? Ed] who I really love. I want to have paid off my student debts and I want to have a few really good friends.

I'd like to be famous either with the pen or the larynx [singing!]. Failing that, a lecturer in religion, sexuality and gender

With a gorgeous woman, in my own house and in a stable job.

It would be nice to have lesbian or gay films released all over the country, not just at a few selected cinemas, and I'd like to see a young version of *Queer as Folk* with girls in it as well as boys, and a gay/lesbian youth magazine.

Where will you be in ten years?

new doors

As I walk through the corridors of my mind
I see many doors.
Doors that are all inviting
Many give a sense of optimism
Many give a fear of excitement
Many give an unnerving
But challenging view of what's laid out
Before me

How frightening it is to have the freedom to choose
My own way of life
How exciting to be able to push those doors
And find a whole new horizon
A scene that's never been seen before
As I walk and enter through different doors
I meet the people I always wanted to meet

How your life can change
By pushing new doors
Seeing people and places
That you've looked for
All your life

anon

9

Dear Diary,

I've been trying to come out to my mum. Well not really come out, I mean I'm only 15 and I'm not gay. Gross. But I keep having these dreams and they are really, really freaking me out…

I'm in an army club and we have to do activities and you are not allowed to quit. This girl and I escape into a room.

Nightmare

Boyz with Boyz.
Girlz with Girlz.
And then we kiss a heart-stopping kiss
Then we are in my room, my bedroom…
Kissing, holding, touching on the bed…
Dad comes in, Brother comes in…
Panic panic

WAKE UP

I wake up crying every time, so scared
Why?

Because I'm gay.

Lee, 17, Yorkshire

In the beginning

You always know the start of something
When you're not quite sure if it's right or wrong
Or maybe you just don't want to know at all.

Like the first time you looked into those eyes.
Those eyes in the face you've spent so long looking at.
If you close your eyes you know you will see that face.
You will tell yourself it's just a crush,
Just a crush.
Infatuation, it won't last long.

Then there's the endless nights of tossing and turning.
No sleep. Desperate.
Desperate to see those eyes.
You speak to yourself.
Infatuation, it won't last long.
It's not love.

But you always know the start of something
When you're not quite sure if it's right or wrong.
Or maybe you just don't want to know at all.

Fran, 21, Avon

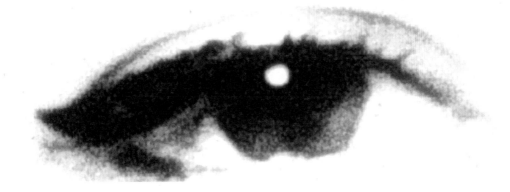

When I was about six I discovered Kylie and then at eight I had feelings for a female teacher and was most disgusted when she got pregnant. I had a big thing for Jenni Garth in *Beverly Hills 90210* when I was about nine or ten. The biggest clue was when I had fantasies about female teachers taking me home and teaching me the ropes when I was 14. At 15 it was the Spice Girls and Lauren Laverne of Kenickie. I was quite happy because girls are more beautiful than boys. I never knew it was 'wrong' until I was 14 and then I realised the reason I wasn't telling my friends was because it was a female teacher I had a crush on.

I did have a crush on my English teacher but I only realised my feelings after I had come out. Everything about my childhood started dropping into place.

I was extremely confused for a long time. I used to fantasise about women and then make myself do it for men too – just to compare and contrast. I wasn't really coping but then I told my friend and discovered that he felt the same. He was feeling for men everything I was feeling for women. I still felt unsure but at least we were going through everything together. I didn't feel so lonely. Then I experimented and fell in love. It took me a while to find out what made me happy.

I had a huge urge to snog my first schoolteacher, one of my mates and the play scheme leader. As I was brought up in a very old-fashioned, homophobic family, I felt dirty and ended up hating myself. I am now happily living with my girlfriend

I always thought boys were idiots. I used to admire girls. The first woman I ever really fell for was my A-level drama teacher. She was so lovely. I can't quite remember what she looked like because for years I never made any eye contact. I couldn't look at her because I was so sure she'd notice how much I liked her. I can tell you every detail about her shoes though.

A female friend took my hand one night. My body tingled all over. My heart was pounding in my chest.

Mel C Mel C Mel C!

What first made you think you fancied girls?

*In the beginning there was beauty

Love didn't begin with my crush on Kylie at five, or deciding that I was gay at ten, or even coming out at fifteen. Love began when I discovered beauty. The day I covered the inside of a cupboard door in pictures of Emma Bunton was the defining moment of my self-discovery and the acceptance of my sexuality. As I stood back and admired that cupboard door for the first time I was truly happy and I decided that this was lesbianism, this pure happiness that was so easy to obtain.

I started to carry around a tiny notebook with the words 'my beautiful little secret' on the front. Inside I traced out quotations by Oscar Wilde, lyrics by Kenickie, anything I considered to be as beautiful as my little secret. And the most perfect pictures of flawless women were kept within its pages.

It's not a secret anymore, and the pictures of Emma Bunton have long since been removed from that cupboard door. But the most beautiful aspect of my life is still that perfect ability to love.

Su Davison is 18. Su says keeping a diary is helpful if you are questioning your sexuality or thinking of coming out

✱ When I was thirteen

When I was 13, I started noticing older girls at school were very interesting and pretty and sophisticated. I thought I wanted to be like them, like my straight friends. But then I met Mel, the deputy head girl who became a close friend. When I saw her in the canteen or school grounds I used to feel hot, sweaty and sort of choked up. I thought I was ill for about four weeks, until my best friend Deb asked me, "What's his name – you're in love aren't you?" Well girl, I can tell you I went home and cried and cried and decided that I didn't really like Mel after all. Yes I definitely wasn't going to be a lesbian, not those horrible crewcut women with moustaches and tattoos and butch gruff voices. Ugh! So I tried to avoid her and things calmed down until about four months later when I again found myself having crushes on female teachers and older girls. Did I deny I was gay? Course I did. All the images of lesbians I'd ever had were scary, negative ones.

Well, after five years of going out with two boys (not for long) and trying to imagine kissing women, I started coming round to the idea of perhaps being bisexual. The problem was I attended a strict all-girls Catholic school and was told what horrible creatures homosexuals were and that any Catholic could not possibly be one. I also attended church a lot and had that view impressed on me even more.

I was in an awful dilemma, what should I do? I decided it was time to venture out into the big wide world so I joined a voluntary organisation called CSV (Community Service Volunteers) who helped me to get voluntary work in Camden, London.

It was a totally new world. After my first two weeks I'd met a few gay people and kissed my first girlfriend… we only stayed together for three months. I expected things would be perfect after I came out, but you really have to work at things, just like any relationship. I still had guilt feelings about being gay, which lasted for the two years I stayed in Camden. I had two girlfriends in that time. One for about a year who taught me a lot and that I couldn't live a lie and pretend I'm something I'm not. It gave me a lot of comfort to go on my first Pride party. It was packed with so many gay men and women, I cried with joy and realised I was not alone.

After two years I decided to go back home to Manchester. When people asked me what I'd been doing for those two years I didn't know what to say but they knew I was a lot happier. One thing led to another and friends guessed and family broached the subject. Through a lot of hardship, tears, love and laughter, I'm out and I'm proud to have become who I want to be. These days I don't get worried if people find out I'm gay. I used to think all lesbians were disgusting pretend men but I've found that they are just like anyone else. And some of the most beautiful people I know are gay.

I know how hard it can be to come out, but believe in yourself and happiness and, whatever struggles you have, you'll be glad you did it in the end.

Kelly, 21, lives in Manchester

Little girl

Little girl on her own
Doesn't know which way to go

Is she straight?
Is she gay?
People stare and stop to say

She'd like to go and tell them all,
The answers they've been waiting for

She's trapped in a game she cannot win
So she lies through her teeth to save her skin

Carla, 15, Avon

15

Thunder

* Kate wants to find a woman to love... but she doesn't think of herself as a lesbian and she struggles in both straight and gay worlds

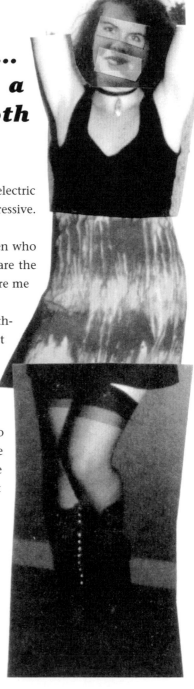

Sitting at my desk, a storm is swirling outside my window. A grumbling moan, an electric flash, and the incessant tapping of rain. I hate thunder, it's so claustrophobic and oppressive. Which kind of reminds me of my sexuality.

I don't know how to explain what I am. I guess I defy classification. There are men who I respect, and many that I don't respect, most of whom I've slept with. Then there are the women that I respect, who are nearly always straight, and there are lesbians, who scare me shitless. Which basically leaves me fantasising over people that I can never have.

I've never been straight, I know that much. When I was six, I declared to my mother that it was silly that women had to marry men, and that I would marry my best friend. Strangely enough, it didn't go down too well. Throughout my childhood, I naively thought that everyone was bisexual; I didn't understand that other people didn't feel like this. So coming to terms with things, for me, conversely meant understanding that other people were different.

I proclaimed my bisexuality aged 15 to a circle of close friends, and consequently to my entire school. Gossip is an odd thing, and for some reason it mattered to people who hardly knew me that I would like to sleep with women. I grew up quickly; there seemed to be little difference between having a sexuality and having sex, and I slept with several men. Some were lovely, some tender, some frightening and some painful, but ultimately it didn't matter; I was saving myself until I was able to make love to a woman. I felt nothing. I tried, I wanted to relax, but I couldn't.

The first girl to touch me was Emily. My first university LGB [lesbian, gay and bisexual society] meeting, my first gay club. Sitting on a sofa in front of everyone in the club, me being kissed by a beautiful woman.

That night we made love, and I was hooked. Emily became the embodiment of all things homosexual, and I idolised her. I slept with other women, but nobody could

make me feel as alive as I had felt that night, with soft skin and smooth hair beneath my trembling fingers. I opened myself to Emily, leaving a knife in a vulnerable wound just waiting to be twisted. And inevitably, it happened. For the first time in my life, emotion and sex had become intertwined, and her rejection hurt excruciatingly. I wandered through the scene alone. I have friends, one or two lesbians and a whole troop of gay men. But sitting week after week in the same pub, without being approached by anyone at all, makes you start to wonder what is wrong with you.

I still go to straight clubs and pubs, with my straight friends. I don't enjoy myself. All the girls there are so much prettier than me. I know that I will not meet anyone who would want to speak to me without a gross ulterior motive. I see men that I find attractive, but when I consider sleeping with them, or even kissing them, it just all seems too unfeasible. Men don't kiss like women, they are not soft and warm; I don't feel a desire to stroke their skin and let myself melt. Men are hard and strong, and I feel that I must always be aware of what they may want next.

Lesbians seem foreign to me. I learnt quickly to avoid telling lesbians that I may be bisexual; the dirtiest word you can use in front of a lesbian – I wanted desperately to belong, and be a member of the group. But despite all my efforts, I could not change my appearance. Whether I go to the pub in jeans, combats or a skirt, I still appear hopelessly feminine, and receive sarcastic comments from girls who have mastered being butch. I have been called the femme de la femme, Kate the straight, and various other things. People say to me that I can't be gay because I look so heterosexual. Most of the time I do not want to be like these other (butch) girls. I want to be a woman, and fall in love with a woman. I want to find somebody gentle and smooth; I don't understand how so many people desire women who make themselves resemble men. I know women like this who are kind and gentle, but there are men who are kind and gentle. Although inside counts above all, it is undeniable that a person's exterior makes a difference.

I want a woman with hair I can feel between my fingers, eyes that glisten through their make-up, legs which stand gracefully in high heels. I want a woman.

I don't feel that I can define myself as a lesbian; I can't play pool for a start, but I simply don't fit into lesbian culture. I am camp as hell, and love my gay friends, but the idea of having a relationship with a lesbian is inconceivable. I want a relationship with a woman. My sexuality does defy labels. Who the hell cares what category I fit into, if I don't? But as I sit here, with thunder rumbling outside my window, I am frightened.

Kate Holmes

Cool to be queer?

Sexuality has finally fallen foul of fashion. In the year 2000 we have reached the final frontier from which a bizarre phenomenon has emerged, the Bandwagon Bisexual. Now fashion, as we are all too aware, is ever-changing. It extends to virtually every aspect of our lives – clothing, style, attitude, posture. Fashion is image and image is everything.

Sexuality is different. Ingrained, innate. Sexuality is as much part of the individual as the colour of your skin. And, you would imagine, equally unique. You're gay. You're straight. You're bisexual. You're confused (aren't we all?). Whatever you are, you are, and while being true to your nature can arouse anything from understanding to distaste to outright hostility, who you are is more or less immutable and, hopefully, uncorruptible.

So, fashion is fashion and sexuality is sexuality and never the twain shall meet. Right?

Wrong. In the past few years, as gay culture moves out of the ghetto and into the heterosexual mainstream, the notion of same-gender attraction has attained a certain credibility, endorsed by the sexually ambiguous antics of celebrities: Hollywood rock-widow Courtney Love, self-styled antichrist superstar Marilyn Manson, Madonna. In their wake a bevy of image-conscious chameleons follow, keen to embrace a lifestyle which requires neither risk nor effort. To them sexuality is little more than an exclusive label, to be worn not lived.

The message is clear, it's cool to be queer, well possibly bisexual, even if you are straight.

All this sounds to me like a cop-out. Some might go so far as to call it offensive. The resolutely gay struggle against everyday bigotry. What gets to me is that people who are 'essentially straight' can sidestep trouble as they are seen as 'essentially normal' in the eyes of the mainstream world. I'm not talking here about those genuinely bisexual people who are stretching the boundaries of identity.

I am surprised that so far there has been so little reaction. Why? Does it have something to do with the widely held view that sexuality is a choice of the individual? This is a fallacy. Sexuality chooses you. In any case, regardless of the way you swing, if you swing at all, it goes without saying the respect is all, even those of you who use your sexuality as fashion statement. A final word of warning. Enter into a relationship with a bandwagon bisexual at your peril. Be vigilant. This seasons's Prada is just a bin-liner waiting to happen.

Natalie

✳ *Norrina writes...*

Working as a youth worker I came into contact with an Asian girl, Yasmin, aged 14. I had known her a year or so before she told me that she thought she might be gay. Yasmin struggled with her sexuality. I supported her in any way I could. In time she felt comfortable identifying as a young lesbian and came out to all her friends. Life was happening for her. I didn't see her for some time but after about 18 months she came to see me. She said that she had something to tell me and I'd be really angry with her. Nervous and anxious, the words would not come out.

I asked her, "What's the worst thing that could happen?" "You'd never speak to me again and you'd think I was stupid," she said. I reassured her that whatever it was, we'd sort it out and I'd be there for her. She then said that she had fallen for a boy, they were going out together and she thought she might be straight. I told her it was fine and to do what she felt comfortable with. Yasmin felt I would disapprove because others had.

This is a common experience for young bisexuals. They are often told that they are 'confused'. But could it be that the young women are not confused but making active choices to be bisexual, lesbian, heterosexual?

auntie fanny
& the agony gang

Q: I think I'm bi... what shall I do?

Nina Be cautious, you have nothing to prove to anyone so don't jump into bed with the first individual you see to prove you are straight/gay. Sleep with those you care for.

Anna Don't think you can't identify with straight people just cos they have different sexual preferences.

Cassie Some people are Bi. Don't think you have to decide on one sex or the other.

Kerry Bi-people shouldn't be afraid to come out as you can belong to both worlds.

Fiona Be yourself and have respect for yourself and your partner.

Kay You don't have to be butch or femme. Don't take shit from anyone. If you are happy with feeling attracted to women and men then there is nothing wrong with defining yourself as bisexual. You are not confused. You are not fickle. It's just how you are. If people say you are sitting on the fence, they are just being ignorant. You don't have to choose between being straight or being lesbian.

Laura It's important to fall in love with a person for who they are regardless of sex. Sometimes finding sexual attraction within a person is not as simple as this. I feel sexuality is a biological thing which you have no control over.

Lindsey Have fun, experiment!

girl2girl

Who do you think you are?

✳ *We are like clothes*

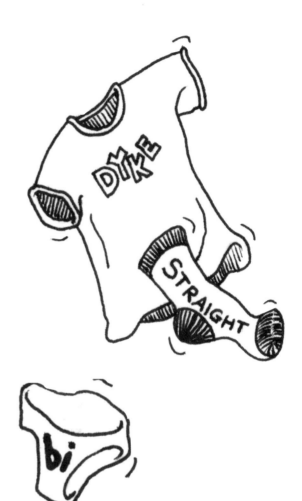

Racked up rail by rail. A monthly treat, trophy of success to be praised and labelled. My mum thinks I'm something out of Marks and Spencer following the suburban line, straight and narrow. I'm a bit of an East End [of Glasgow] girl really, a bit scruffy but in a quirky kind of way. The truth is I'm probably a bit of a BHS, you know, trying hard but not quite getting there. If only my Mum knew the truth, accepted the truth, had seen me out in my East End bars, modelling my success. Being me.

That's the funny thing about being out. Is it or isn't it something to be provided? I began providing my own style at 16. But was it my own style? I think I epitomised the codes. You know, the checked shirt and boots, the biker jacket, the classic V-neck and now the combats and tight long-sleeved tops. We all use it to satisfy our needs. We mix to assist others, to pull, to be part of the cause. You need that fashion code, you hang on to it. It makes you feel like you are not the only one; you belong. You don't know anyone to talk to. I certainly didn't in my TopShop school. You dress to impress, improve, prove. Just in case anyone notices that checked shirt and boots and thinks, "Maybe, just maybe."

Nicola Wood, 21, lives in Glasgow. She studies social sciences at university and started writing four years ago. She has had poetry published and two of her plays have been performed in Aberdeen

Cyberchick chats with Lisa about being bi
Topic: I'm not sitting on the fence

> **Hi Lisa!**

Hi there Cyberchick.

> **Tell me, what influenced you in your decision to be bisexual?**

I have identified myself (at least to myself) as bisexual since age 15. I couldn't say that anything in particular influenced me. I knew for some time before that that I had feelings for both girls and boys, but found these feelings confusing and upsetting. After looking at advice sites on the internet, I learned that there was such a thing as 'bisexuality', and it made sense to think of myself in that way. It wasn't a decision as such, I just realised that to be honest with myself, I had to admit and accept the fact that I experience attraction to members of both sexes.

> **What makes you identify as bisexual rather than say, straight or lesbian?**

If I was looking for a partner, their gender wouldn't make a significant difference. To say that i was lesbian or straight would deny my true feelings.

> **What would you say to people who suggest that being bisexual is just sitting on the fence or not taking responsibility for yourself?**

I would say that I didn't know there was a fence. That sounds stupid but what I mean is, I don't see why the issue of sexuality should be one of taking sides – people should be left alone to love who they love, and not be judged for it. I'm taking the responsibility to be individual and not

Topic: do not accept the LIFE_STAGES.TXT file. it is a virus. delete it if you reci **set by:**

#Girl2Girl

Nickname	I	F	Hostname
Lisa			Littlegirl@ror
CYBERCHICK			CYBER@virgin

Inputline

P B U ab

ircleuser(....) talking to #Cyberchick

t n i p s m l k

Op	Kick	Msg
DeOp	Ban	Cping
Whois	BanKick	Query

be forced into the neatly labelled boxes ('gay', 'straight') that some people seem to depend upon to understand other people. If it was suggested that by saying I'm bisexual, I am denying my 'true homosexual feelings', then I would say that just isn't true. I don't deny my homosexual feelings, and I also don't deny my heterosexual feelings. I wouldn't mind being gay or straight, but that's not the way it has turned out.

> **If you are currently in a relationship, tell me a bit about it.**

I am in a wonderful relationship with a lovely girl called Debbie who is the same age as me and also a student. I am totally monogamous and I think that sleeping with someone else, male or female, is plain cheating, and greedy. Debbie is a lesbian but says she doesn't mind that I'm bisexual because she trusts me. We enjoy going to both straight and gay pubs and clubs together.

> **Cool. Maybe we'll see you around.**

Maybe!

< Cyberchick has left the chatroom >

Lisa is 20 and studying sociology at Cardiff University. "In my spare time I enjoy playing bass guitar and trombone and am generally very interested in music. I love going to the cinema and playing pool... This sounds like a job application!"

No longer hidden by a wardrobe

Coming out.
What an over-rated piece of shit
although definitely painful.
Sure I don't mind being gay.
Sure I don't mind the narrow-minded
dickheads who think they rule the world.
Sure I don't mind going to bed at night
wanting to be 'normal'.
Come on, would you enjoy the torment?
It wouldn't be so bad if there
was someone to share my feelings with
someone to hold and cuddle at night.
As if I enjoy the pure insanity of homophobic
teenagers who think that
just because they're female it must mean that
I fancy them.
As if my taste is that fucking bad.
One of these days I'll scream

very loudly
in the hope that someone will hear me
and come to my aid.
There's obviously an unwritten rule that
automatically means people are
homophobic, prejudiced arseholes
to anyone who is even the slightest bit different.
They must think that because I'm gay
I have a horrible personality and a
sick mind underneath my exterior.
Although having said that it seems
that my exterior isn't average either.
Apparently no female around with the
exception of me has short spiky
hair and combats.
As if.

Hannah, 16

* I think I always knew

I think I always knew somewhere inside I was gay, but I thought it was just feelings of friendship for girlfriends and best girlfriends. It wasn't until I was about 12 that I began to realise other girls weren't quite the same.

Then my sister came out as bisexual, then later a lesbian. I couldn't understand it. I found it disgusting! It was very confusing because school was very homophobic. There weren't any positive images or any images at all of gay people. I thought it was unnatural and abnormal. I loved my sister but I was angry with her for being different and freaky.

I think it took me longer to come to terms with my own sexuality because my sister had already been there, done that. Perversely, my sibling rivalry with my sister made it harder to admit that I fancied women, because I did not want to be the same as her. I was really triumphant that I'd slept with a women when I was 16, when I knew she hadn't, though I didn't really enjoy it. That one bad experience with a girl made me think that I didn't fancy women and I was still blocking off my feelings even though I was still having crushes on girls.

There was heavy stigma and homophobia at school. At my secondary school they used to call me Lezzie Lizzie. It made me angry and confused because boys tended to call me it and I didn't understand why, because I fancied boys. I used to get upset, but sort of laugh and say no I'm not.

I didn't really have many people to talk to, just my sister. I coped by locking myself in my room, listening to music and reading. I thought I was a lesbian but at the same time I was having crushes on boys. I felt I had to prove something, so I tried to get a boyfriend. After all, everyone else had one. After my first snog with a man I bragged about it to everyone.

College opened up a whole new world to me. I decided I was bisexual, although I was not very open about it. Since I left college I've been going to a gay youth group and feel comfortable with being bisexual now.

Liz, 19

* Reluctantly gay

It is much easier being out at university than at school doing A-levels. But what I find most interesting about women between the age of 18 and 20 is a real reluctance to declare themselves bisexual or gay. I'm the president of the under-graduate body at my college and so talk to a lot of students about coming out etc. Yet time and time again, they have secret relationships and always maintain that they are just having a relationship now and this is not necessarily for life. The standard line is "My sexuality is not defined by a specific gender but a person." This seems more PC and easier to handle and I am rare for being sure enough at this age to be 'gay' (though never lesbian). The whole thing is intensely private and being out and proud is now considered very passé. And so it all links back to an anxiety and shame that is just called something else.

Ruth Hunt is 20 and in her second year studying English at Oxford University, where she is president of the student union at St Hilda's College

auntie fanny
& the agony gang

Q: Help! I am questioning my sexuality and feel confused – what can I do?

Nina   Follow your heart.

Anna   Live your life for you. Just do what you think's best.

Kay   Don't be in a rush to label yourself.

Cassie   Go with the flow. Don't let it affect you. Enjoy it, don't try to destroy it. It's part of you.

Kerry   You are what you are. Enjoy. Experiment with your sexuality. If you try to deny your sexuality you will never be truly happy.

Laura   Don't listen to bullies. Pity them for being narrow-minded. Don't let them crush your dreams, and remember you are not alone.

Fi   Don't make hasty decisions, be open-minded and only tell people that you feel comfortable with.

Because the heart isn't where we think it is

This isn't the only story I have to tell. After all, we are all a collection of stories. Everyday we reinvent ourselves, remember our heroic days and those not so heroic, those triumphant and not so triumphant. Some, being very attached to their stories, recall page after page. Other take pains to forget, or rip out pages, chapters, whole books. I was a very determined person at 16. I promised myself I'd never be someone else's cliché. Is everyone else thinking the same at 16? This is the story my parents will ignore, or at least try to. This is the story my parents didn't want me to write. This isn't the glorious vision of the writer-daughter they had in mind.

I sit in a box every day. Straight for my parents, unaffected for my friends, romantic for my lover. I won't fit into the box you have ready for me. Even if there were some tidy, neat, little packaging that I could be placed into, I wouldn't know or accept it. There are no victims in my story and I won't be one for you. You pretend to understand, but I don't think you do.

I'd like not to have been a cliché. I'd like to tell you that at 13 I was content with who I was, that I didn't think every day should have been my last. This is the chapter I wanted to rip out of my heart and soul. I realised that what I felt all my life had a name, but I couldn't and wouldn't utter it. I'm trying to be truthful, I'm trying to remember how it happened and how it felt, but the memory has faded the ink on the pages and I'm not sure if that's choice or just how it is.

I wanted to protect my father from the truth, I tried so hard for his affections all my life. But my Asian family extends further than the four walls of our home. As a child it was acceptable for me to play with the boys, act like the boys, cut my hair and play in the mud, but as I got older the questions came – fast and furious. "When will you grow your hair? No one will marry you with short hair." Hair is a virtue in the Sikh faith. Mine, cut short, left nothing to their imaginations.

This is the hardest story I have to tell. I have often used the soothing sounds of my words to hide myself from the world and from you. Now I have nothing to hide behind and my words are forcefully lucid on this page. I fell in love with a woman at 17. I loved her more than my body could take. I loved her in private. Afraid of watchful eyes I could never take her hand as we walked or kiss her neck on the bus.

We are full of contradictions. I am 18 now but still today some of that 13-year-old, scared and trapped. But mostly I am free of that person. My parents are yet to find out what the rest of the world already knows. I am gay.

Joni, 18, lives in east London and is about to go to university

Coming to terms with my

SEXUALITY

Coming to terms with my sexuality was very difficult. At school I was bullied due to my size, colour and because I'm adopted. I was lucky because I had parents I could talk to. They talked to the teachers. To be honest it didn't help much, but at least I had someone I could talk to about the bullying. So when I admitted to myself I was gay, I thought bloody hell, what else could go wrong in my messed-up life?

I tried to ignore my feelings towards girls because I thought it would cause more trouble. My life was messed up enough. I had a bad crush on my English teacher. Would do anything to see her, even make out I needed extra help. I didn't fancy other girls so I just pretended it was a crush.

The bullying got bad and I changed schools. At my new school I fell in love with a girl in my year. I couldn't really ignore it, pretend or lie to myself. How come all my crushes were on girls or women teachers? I felt like ending it all. Couldn't really face being gay.

I saw a number for Gay Switchboard [see Info zone for 'switchboards' or helplines]. I phoned up hundreds of times and stayed silent. One day I said, "I want to end it all." The woman on the phone was really nice. We got talking and she gave me the number of a youth group for people like me and offered to meet me. I was so nervous. I thought she was going to be ugly and fat. I thought all gay women were ugly and fat and looked like men. I was so wrong. She was beautiful. Long brown hair, deep brown eyes and her clothes were really normal.

She took me to the youth group. I was really nervous and I nearly didn't go. I'm glad I did as you could say it's saved my life. After a while I came to terms with it and accepted it as part of me. I won't change who I am due to someone's bigotry and hatred of what they think is so-called abnormal.

I first came out as bi because it was more accepted, and later on I came out as gay. I had to be true to myself. Coming out was right for me at the time I chose. But don't do it until you feel ready and comfortable with your own sexuality. Be confident.

Becky is 17 and lives in Bradford

My journey into a queer world

Summer '98 I was blissfully suppressing my lesbian tendencies by entering into another doomed straight relationship. Well what else was I to do? – there was no chance of me finding a girlfriend in my straight world! So I was just making the most of starting a new job at a nightclub, where my new boyfriend also worked.

Then I was introduced to my manager – Sam, an actual lesbian! I was instantly fascinated by her, but she never talked about being gay, and my boyfriend thought it was odd I asked so many questions about her. We became friends though. She lived with her girlfriend of seven years, and when they decided to go on a weekend break, they asked me and my boyfriend if we would look after their cats.

Sam and her girlfriend seemed to have a very solid relationship, even though Sam never really talked much about her private life. Her girlfriend regularly turned up late at night to meet Sam from work.

I started to confide in Sam about my relationship problems with my boyfriend, as she was his friend. We used to laugh together about how utterly useless he was, especially when he got the sack for drug taking. He stayed at my flat after he lost his job, and I grew more and more resentful of him. He drank lots and never had any money – I even had to buy my own Valentine's present.

I had a lesbian friend in Ireland who I wrote to regularly. I had confessed my confusion over my sexuality to her, but had done nothing more about it. After speaking with her I decided to finish with my boyfriend, and arranged to visit her in Ireland. When I was there I visited some gay bars and decided it was about time I dealt with my sexuality.

I ended up sleeping with my friend – the first woman I had slept with. It didn't feel strange at all – just so much easier and more natural.

I returned to London to try and find myself a girlfriend, but didn't really know where to start. At this point I considered myself bisexual, simply because I couldn't explain why I had had more than one boyfriend.

A couple of weeks later, I went on a staff pub crawl in Covent Garden. Everyone got very drunk and silly. Various members of staff were copping off with each other. I had my camera with me, and people were performing interesting stunts to get their photo taken. Someone grabbed it and told me to pose. I grabbed Sam, who just happened to be next to me, and told her to give me a kiss for the camera. I was expecting a peck, but got a full-on snog [Sam's on the right of the pic]. The rest, shall we say, is history.

Sam and I were inseparable for the rest of the evening, and ended up back at my place. She had a guilt attack and eventually went back to her flat (with her knickers in her pocket).

The next few days at work were awkward. I thought Sam regretted the whole thing, as she was avoiding me. When we were alone though, she flirted with me, and she gave me a kiss goodbye at the end of each shift. We also started phoning each other. She confessed that her relationship with her girlfriend was on the rocks, and that they were really more like friends.

One Sunday evening she called to say that she had finished with her girlfriend and moved into the flat above the nightclub. I dropped everything and drove over to stay with her and we've been together ever since. We were the controversy of the moment for a while – me seducing my lesbian boss and stealing her from her girlfriend.

A year later we are planning our future together. I came out to my family. My parents are fine about it, only a bit embarrassed, and Sam and I visit once a week. My Nana thinks it's great and tells me about lesbians she knew in the war and how horrible homophobes are. She has invited us to a family reunion in July where I will get to meet other gay relatives, like my dad's cousin who has lived with his boyfriend for 20 years.

Now I feel like I've got to make up for lost time – I spent years being the only gay person in Berkhamsted (though a few of my friends have confessed their gay encounters to Sam!) and got fed up of going to straight venues and being harassed by straight men.

I realise I am definitely a lesbian, and that I went out with men to try and prove to myself that I could be straight. I am on work experience with a gay newspaper and am about to graduate. Sam and I are moving to Brighton, where I just want to do my bit for the gay community.

Rebecca Greig is 21 and was brought up in Hertfordshire. She now lives with her girlfriend, and has just moved to Brighton from London where she was on work experience with the Pink Paper

Transgender tale

Although there is a stereotype that says tomboys turn into lesbians, sometimes they turn into men. Here's Andrew's story of the transition from female to male...

Anyone who claims to be normal is conning themselves. What's normal about uniformity? It is natural for variety to exist.

I am 18 years old and will not be deciding to return to living as female, ever. Transitioning for me is not an option, it was/is a necessity. The feeling that I should present myself to the world differently to how I would be expected to, as a physically female person, was not 'a phase'. I always, in one way or another, felt different, if not always unhappy. I always knew people believed I was a girl, but that label was too clear cut, I felt, to be applied to me.

I remember clearly an occasion at playgroup, aged three years. I finally got my turn to ride the toy tractor. When the whistle was blown for the next person's turn I looked up to see a girl waiting. I kept going, thinking to myself, "Why should I give it up for a girl? Girls don't need to know how to ride tractors!" Still, justice was done. I let her have her go.

At that time I lived in Norfolk. My next stage was school. Unfortunately I started at a private girls' school, where ballet lessons were compulsory – I hated every minute, but there was no mercy, until...

My parents divorced and I moved with my mum and brothers to Dorset, where I started at a local primary school. I played on the football 'B' team and got on well with the people there.

At secondary school, things generally went downhill. Any support I received at primary school for enjoying rugby and the company of boys soon disappeared. I didn't ever wish to shave my legs. A fact which caused great amusement to my co-pupils. My so-called cross-dressing was not popular. I hated wearing a bra, let alone having to go through the procedure of having it fitted, so I opted out of that. Of course, the only conclusion that could be drawn at that time, by myself included, was that I must be a butch lesbian. It was the only identity I knew of that would let me express my masculine qualities.

Two nights in February 1996 discredited any previous conclusions I had drawn about the meaning of my gender expression. I watched a two-part documentary featuring three people transitioning from female to male. One person was exactly my age and already had the full support of his family and friends recognising his gender as male. I was scared, but hopeful, though my future seemed all too far away and virtually unobtainable.

My mum has been great. At first she tried to say she had the same feelings when she was my age. Gradually she saw it wasn't going away, though she privately hoped it would. Since I began taking testosterone I think she has felt it is a more definite issue.

But am I not just a lesbian, trying to conform to the heterosexual ideal? No. There is nothing acceptable to society about messing with nature.

Society will never be satisfied with the results of my future surgery. They tell me I will never be a 'real' man. There is the assumption that gay couples try to simulate their relationships to be like heterosexual couples i.e. that one is the man and one is the woman. It is also assumed that everyone who transitions will take on a heterosexual identity. This is not always the case. Although someone may turn initially to the gay communitiy for a place to express their gender identity and may be attracted to women, it is perfectly possible, after transitioning, to be attracted only to men.

So if I am attracted to men, why did I bother transitioning? Because my mind is male. Because I would not want the female qualities of my body to be liked or desired. Because I dislike the female qualities of my body and because I need my true identity to be expressed.

There are those in the transgendered community, including myself, who believe gender identity is not confined to the realms of man/woman. There are people who do not fit such categories. Some would say they are a blend of both, others would say they are sometimes male, sometimes female. Others still would not describe themselves as either.

As the term bisexual relies upon there being just two genders, some feel it is necessary to use instead the term pansexual. This shows recognition that people can be attracted to others, not on the basis that they are either man or woman, but for the person they are.

Andrew James is 18 and studying at college in Dorset
For advice and support on transgender issues, see the contacts in the Info zone

auntie fanny
& the agony gang

Q: I don't feel like a girl...
I want to change sex

Anna   Think long and hard till you are 100% sure.

Sam   Do what makes you happy. Your body. Your life.

Lindsey   If it would help your self-esteem then seek medical information and query whether it is possible. However, changing your body does not make you straight, or equal in the straight world.

Lee   Think really seriously about it. Girls are best but if you feel that you should really be a man then do what makes you feel comfortable.

I can't tell

How can I admit to what I have denied for so long
Sharing with others what I can't accept myself
It would be like throwing meat to lions
And expecting them not to rip it into pieces
I know I would be hailed a hero by some
And even admired by others
But I would disgust the ones that mean the most
So how can I tell?
Maybe time will make it go away
If I wait long enough maybe it won't taunt me
But time is simply a counter
Reminding me how long I've already wasted
I may seem confident on the outside
But inside I'm scared and weak.

Jen Ashton, 19, wrote this when she was at college. Because she had denied it in the past, she felt that telling people about herself now would make them think their friendship had been a lie

Escape

Trapped being a person you know you are not
It protects everyone else, who you care for a lot.
Life'd be so much easier if you could just suppress –
Think of the hurt for you to openly confess.
The fact is you can't carry on this way,
Feelings build up and get stronger each day.
You feel alone and misunderstood
You need to talk, Oh if only you could
Then out of the blue that day will arrive
The burden is lifted, you feel so alive
It's all a bit scary but exciting and new
A whole new beginning, living your life for you

Anna Stimpson, 20, Coventry

God made me like this

✳ Norrina Rashid talks to Naz and Salima about their lives, sexuality and religion. They live together in Bradford and have been partners for nearly two years. Naz is 19 and Salima is 21

Norrina: *Tell me a bit about your families.*

Naz: I've got two sisters and a brother. They all live at home with Mum and Dad.

Norrina: *Salima, what's your family like?*

Salima: Ooh, they're very nice, the perfect Muslim family. Not. My family live in Glasgow, that's where I grew up. I loved growing up in my family. It was really nice, a loving family. I don't know what I think now.

Norrina: *What happened to change things?*

Salima: Me and my big mouth. I was upset, crying my eyes out. My mum was trying to find out what was wrong. I couldn't tell her and didn't know what she would think.

Naz: At least it proved she cared. She wanted to know why you were crying

Salima: Oh yeah, and telling everyone your daughter's dead proves you care, does it?

Norrina: *So your mum told everyone you had died?*

Salima: Aye. When she realised I wasn't the perfect daughter anymore.

Naz: She did try to help at first.

Norrina: *I'm confused. What happened?*

Salima: I lost loads of weight and was bulimic. I couldn't sleep and took an overdose. I just kept crying. My mum was really nice. She was so nice, it just came out. I told her I was in love with Sheila and Sheila had left me. My Mum didn't say anything. I don't even remember how it happened. I told her everything… that we loved each other and were going to live together. My mum just walked off. She didn't speak to me for weeks. It was kind of weird in the house.

Norrina: *Did things sort themselves out?*

Salima: Not really. I came home from school one day and all these men from the mosque were there. I knew something was going on. I went straight to my room. My stupid little sister was there. It was one big fuck-up. My mum told me to come down. She started ranting and raving about jinn [a spirit in Islamic theology with supernatural powers] and told me they were gonna get rid of the jinn. It was awful, I ran away about a year after that.

Norrina: *Do you believe in jinn?*

Naz: Sort of.

God made

Norrina: What do you believe about it?

Naz: I believe that there is a higher being. God. Therefore I believe in evil spirits and that evil spirits can take over your body and make you do things.

Norrina: What sort of things?

Salima: Turn you into a lesbian!

Naz: Stop being stupid. I think they can make you kill people and stuff.

Norrina: Have you ever wondered if you have been affected by jinn?

Naz: No, because I don't hurt anyone. But it's really hard for me. I mean, Salima's not really a Muslim.

Salima: You sound like those hypocritical Muslims! What do you mean, I'm not really a Muslim?

Naz: I'm not a hypocrite. What I mean is, you don't practise Islam. You don't pray and you drink. I pray. I read the Koran. I live an Islamic lifestyle.

Salima: So what about when we're in bed? That's not very Islamic, is it?

Naz: Yeah, That's different. I pray and bathe before and after sex. But we can't get married so I can't do anything else, can I?

Norrina: Naz, you were saying it's really hard for you?

Naz: It is hard for me. I always knew I was different and I tried really hard. I prayed and this is where I have been led. It's not that I chose to be gay. It's the way God made me.

Norrina: What about your Muslim friends? Do they give you a hard time?

me like this

Naz: My real friends aren't bothered. They know I live with Salima. Sometimes they ask stupid questions like, how do I know I am really gay if I've not gone all the way with a guy? But I don't believe in sex before marriage.

Norrina: What about the Muslim community as a whole?

Naz: I don't introduce myself as a lesbian. I just say I love Salima. But I know really they would not approve. But then neither would the Christian, Sikh or Jewish religious communities. People just think Muslims are worse.

Norrina: What about your parents?

Naz: My mum knows. I told her. She doesn't understand. There's no real word for gay in our language. She thinks I'm a man. She told me God would not forgive me.

Norrina: How does that make you feel?

Naz: Scared.

Norrina: How do you manage to feel OK about being gay and a practising Muslim?

Naz: I believe God made me like this. My life was mapped out before I was born. So long as I don't do anything bad I'll be OK.

Norrina: What about you, Salima?

Salima: I don't give a shit. Tell them to look at themselves first. They walk round like they are top Muslims. They go to hajj [pilgrimage to Mecca], pray, do all that stuff. But they might treat their wives, sisters and daughters really bad. I just get on with my life.

See the Info zone for details of organisations for lesbian and gay Muslims and other religions

Seek and ye shall find

*Julia Collar answers back to the myths spread by Christian fundamentalists about lesbians

Anti-lesbian myth one:

God will punish you for being lesbian or bisexual

All religions are founded upon the principles of love and responsible relationships. As long as you love in truth and honesty and are not reckless with people, then I find it hard to believe that any God would punish or reject you, regardless of who your lover is. Strength and true faith comes from knowing the arguments: argue your case with yourself to reconcile yourself.

Practically every religion has a denomination or group that welcomes gay members to their congregations. There is a lot of support, guidance and affirmation to be found for the faithful. Jesus said, "Seek and ye shall find." Religion is often about community; find one that will welcome you in and enter the debate with good company.

Anti-lesbian myth two:

The Bible says homosexuality is a bad thing

What the Bible tells us is very different from what the Bible has been interpreted as saying. St Paul is often quoted as condemning homosexuality as well as the practices of other non-Christian religions around him. But he was speaking for himself and not on behalf of Jesus, who never once spoke of homosexuality, let alone condemned it. Anti-gay beliefs were made up by powerful men who felt they should suppress their bodily desires in their search for spirituality and God.

Anti-lesbian myth three:

Homosexuals are sick, weak and depraved and are being led away from God

I can think of a lot of far worse things that drag heterosexuals away from God than loving someone of the same sex so why should *we* be seen as weak? Many of the people who think this crap have been found to have had homosexual experiences themselves.

The truth is that by refusing to squash ourselves into the heterosexual 'norm', we threaten to rock the very bastions of society: family, gender roles, relationships, fucking and so on. These areas are very dear to the church who think that they are supposed to enable us to better love one another and to come closer to God. Because we are trying to live our own way and remake our families, we pose a direct challenge to their human authority (not divine authority). The churches think the faith they have is superior so they try to make us into anxious victims by calling

us depraved heretics.

I saw a documentary once about Nazi Germany. Apparently they believed that, if you can control people's bodies, you can control them utterly. That has really stuck with me because it is a horrific truth. I'm not saying that all Christians against homosexuality are fascist but I think the Church's stance on sexuality is about control. If Section 28 is repealed it would mean that the Church would lose one of its most effective means of control.

Anti-lesbian myth four:

Lesbian and gay people shouldn't be ordained – they would be a corrupting influence on the young

This is based on such a stereotype. Paedophiles are one thing (most of them are straight anyway) and lesbians and gays are another. Anyway, I don't think you can make someone gay just like that.

Oh yes and that 'AIDS is a punishment from God' thing is just another way to keep us fearful. I really can't see how they can still keep saying this as AIDS is such a big problem all over the world now [not just among gay men].

I often think, what would religion be like if it was tolerant and even embraced us? My guess is that it would be no different and that God would breathe a huge sigh of relief and shout "About Time Too!"

Although faith is ultimately a personal thing between the heart and mind of a believer and their God, we do need people fighting to achieve a place for us in religious institutions. These are the people who have clout, who will make a difference for us, who have status and learning and will strive to liberate us. We should have the choice whether or not to join them.

Julia Collar has been studying religious studies at Lampeter College, University of Wales. She says she is a 'theist' as she believes in a God but has moved away from her Christian roots

For religious groups sympathetic to lesbians and bisexuals, see Info zone

girl2girl

Friends and family

young lesbians life

you are not alone

out and proud

use support

no one has the right to disrespect you

go out and meet people

love yourself

eat your greens!

speak your mind

be yourself

insanity is a virtue, normality is a virus

always respect yourself

never feel forced to conform

scene life can be fun but be careful

Emma, Yorkshire

love and respect yourself

i's OK to be gay

feel comfortable with your sexuality

enjoy life, be happy

tell all!

It's good to be around similar people without them thinking I'm dodgy or something. Without the group, I think I wouldn't be able to be myself and I'd be quieter and less confident. The first time I went I was only 14 and I recognised some people and went away and burst into tears. The piece of advice I would give someone if they were going to the group for the first time would be brace yourself!

The first time I went, I wasn't really nervous because a friend took me. I'm always confident with new people but I think I still would have found it hard to go by myself. My advice would be to bite the bullet, just go for it.

The group I go to is amazing. I've met some really great friends there and my world be duller without them. Before I came out, the group was a lifeline for me. Breathing space where I didn't have to pretend any more. I used to feel myself physically relax when I came through the door.

It's made me more confident, more than other teenagers the same age as me. I have had to find things out about myself and my feelings earlier than most people have to.

It's one of the best things you'll ever do. You get to meet people you wouldn't usually meet.

I'm more confident with strangers because I'm now at ease with myself. I know my own mind on lots of subjects other people my age haven't thought about. I have better relationships with adults. One of my best friends is 68!

What's so great about the youth group?

For being me

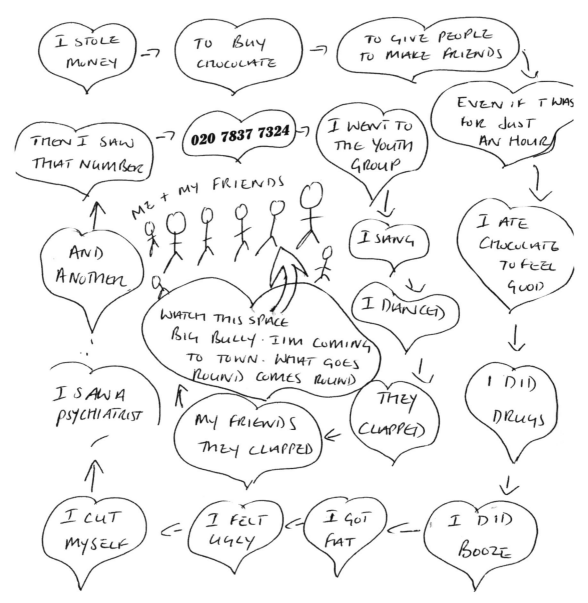

Heather, 17   For your nearest youth group or helpline, check out the Info zone at the back of the book

More lesbians in Runcorn than just me!

✳ *Norrina Rashid interviews Zoey who is just 15 and lives with her mother and her 11-year-old "annoying Batman-wannabe brother" in Runcorn. She goes to a local youth group which her school counsellor told her about*

Norrina: Tell me about your family and friends.

Zoey: I live in a nice quiet estate and a lot of the people who live here are a bit posh. None of them know that I am gay but everyone keeps themselves to themselves so I don't think they ever will. My Mum is really cool. She had me when she was 18 so we're close, like best friends. My brother's a bit thick. No matter how obvious I make it that he's got a dyke for a sister he still doesn't get it, no matter how many pictures of Anna Ryder Richardson I leave lying around! I was shocked that my friends took the news so well. All they could say was 'cool'. That made me feel a whole lot better.

Norrina: What made you question your sexuality?

Zoey: I can pick out the tell-tale signs from the age of three. I remember when I was at nursery there was a helper I really liked. I cried and cried when she left. After millions of things like this happening I finally realised I was gay at the famous wedding of my Uncle Jonathan – Saturday 19 April 1997, I can even remember the date. I was 13. I was staying at the bride's mum's house experiencing my last few hours of heterosexuality, getting my pink frilly brides-maid's dress ready. I'm telling you, I was not impressed. It wasn't until the wedding that I met the chief bridesmaid. Corny as this may sound, the rest was a bit of a daze. I don't remember when it was when I actually thought, Oh my God, I fancy the bridesmaid! The day went well – up until the meal, when I met her boyfriend, the most ugliest Where's Wally lookalike ever. I hated him with a passion. They got married a week later. When I look back I don't know what I saw in her – she was at least 35. But first love is always with you.

Norrina: What did you feel when you first accepted you were a lesbian?

Zoey: When I finally realised I was so relieved. I felt I could relax and let my hair down properly. I was a bit of a tomboy until I was 14. I played football with the boys and wouldn't be seen dead in anything other than my Man United football kit. That changed when I met Kerry, the youth worker. I thought, right, this is the first proper lesbian I have ever met and this is how I must dress. For about four months I had a Kerry lookalike phase. After that I just decided that I should be myself, cos that's who I am. My own character began to show and I make my own decisions in my own way. My role models are George O'Dowd (Boy George) and Ellen Degeneres because they both had to deal with an awful lot of criticism and managed to overcome it. Marilyn Monroe is just fab! Her life is tragic and she just pushed through.

Norrina: How did you come to terms with your sexuality?

Zoey: I wasn't confused. I just thought, I fancy women instead of men; so what. My attitude was different at different times. I may have been truthful to myself but that doesn't mean I coped. I bottled everything up and about a year later I developed an eating disorder. I lost a couple of stone. I was in a mess. I hadn't come out. I was terrified of what people would think. When I came out to Mum last year I just gradually began eating again without even knowing it and I have never looked back.

Norrina: How important is the youth group to you?

Zoey: It was funny when I told my school counsellor I was a lesbian because I couldn't bring myself to say the words so I just said: "I've got more in common with Zoe Tate than just the name." She smiled and I burst out laughing. She told me about the group. It helps me a lot. I saw there were more lesbians in Runcorn than just me.

Norrina: What's the worst thing anyone has ever said to you about your sexuality?

Zoey: I was at my friend Paul's 18th birthday party. He was talking to his Uncle John. It went like this:

Uncle John: So which one of your mates do you fancy, Paul?

Paul: None of them really.

Uncle John: I'd go after Zoey, if I was you, Paul.

Paul: I can't, Zoey's a lesbian.

Uncle John: Is she? What a waste.

Some people may think that's not so bad but I find it really offensive. Just to think that I am a waste of a person because I fancy women and not men. It's ridiculous.

Norrina: Have you ever been bullied?

Zoey: Luckily I've never had any form of homophobic abuse. Before I came out I was quite popular in school. My grades are always good and I'm quite attractive and everybody knew me. I count myself lucky because there are people in my school who got the complete opposite. My tip for anyone being bullied is never put up with it. Don't blame yourself and don't take any of what they say to heart.

Norrina: What's the nicest thing anyone has ever said?

Zoey: A lot of my friends are fascinated. They say things like: Cool, you've kissed another girl. Wow, that's dead good!

Norrina: Do you think your experiences have made you stronger?

Zoey: The way I see it, you are immunised against something and your immune system gets stronger against it. People throw comments and remarks at you and it gets easier each time. You get stronger. When I was about 12, the slightest remark which was not even directed at me would have probably scarred me for life. Now I just ignore what people say or defend myself and hurl a load of abuse back at them. I'm more confident than ever.

Sexreality

When it hit home there was something I knew,
God, I'm a lesbian what do I do?
I tried to ignore it and go the other way,
But I couldn't escape the fact that I'm gay.
Lots of confusion spinning in my head,
Should I really be wanting to take a woman to bed?

I tried to be straight, had to pretend,
Then I decided that sex with a man must end.
After some years I'd figured what I was all about,
Now I needed someone to whom I could come out.

I didn't know of any groups for people my age,
Inside I was screaming my head in a rage.
Then it popped out one sunny day,
I let someone know I was gay.

Then a meeting was arranged with a woman named Kerry,
She was very nice, quite jolly and merry.
She spoke of a group, young people on the same track,
Since then I've been happy, now there's no looking back.

Nina

Somewhere to chill out & chat

* An insider's report on the First Out youth group, just one of many across the country

Young people come to the centre to meet friends who are like them and be somewhere that feels totally OK. Perhaps they might find a girlfriend or boyfriend, get information and advice or just chill out and talk. They talk about where to find jobs, whether to leave home, homophobia at school, what happened when someone had just come out to family and friends, what to say to someone you fancy, how to break up, what Pride was like, exams, exams and more exams, anti-depressants, how homophobic someone's sister is, what happened in Streetlife (a local club) on Saturday, the weekend trip and where to go to have a good time.

Love Macho! Champ fighter is gay!

'Ghetto girl' in directorship job

'Lad' in the Ladies –umbrella drama
"I thought she was a young man" said Edith Smith aged 85

What are your **Misconceptions** of lesbians, gay men and bisexuals?

being **gay** is a part of us

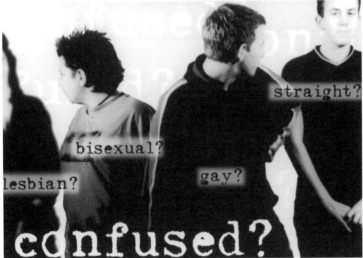

straight?

bisexual?

lesbian?

gay?

confused?

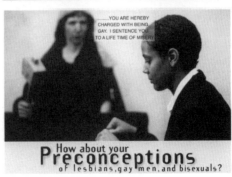

.........YOU ARE HEREBY CHARGED WITH BEING GAY. I SENTENCE YOU TO A LIFE TIME OF MISERY

How about your **Preconceptions** of lesbians, gay men, and bisexuals?

First Out is a gay, lesbian and bisexual youth group for under-25s that meets every week at the Leicester Lesbian, Gay and Bisexual Centre. Soft Touch are a lesbian, gay and bisexual arts group in Leicester who have produced the work shown here.

To reach your nearest group – or a helpline that can find it for you – turn to the Info zone at the back

Alis shouted 'I am gay!'
to the whole school, in a play she wrote herself

Making a drama out of it

When I was seven I was attracted to girls. I thought it was the boys who were usually attracted to girls. But I am so that's that. When I was 11 I discovered words and thought I was bisexual because I liked boys too.

I'm not too keen on labels but now, if I'm asked, I call myself gay or lesbian. Labels restrict you, they stop you from keeping your options open. Straight people like you to have labels – perhaps it makes them feel safer, it's easier to understand, to know you are one thing or another.

I suppose the gay community likes labels so we can identify each other. It made me feel good when I said I was gay. I felt proud, here to stay. But you also get stereotypes, like lesbians with shaved heads and big boots and, er, a labyris tattooed on their arm. I like to dress comfortable. I have always worn my hair short but I recently had extensions and when I was out in the gay village with my friends people said I had gone femme. They take it for granted you are gay if you have short hair.

I've been on *GayTime TV*, a teenage programme *Sort It*, and *Tonight with Trevor Macdonald* to talk about what it is like being bullied at school because of your sexuality. I've spoken at conferences too. It was after I had been having a bad time at school because of bullying. I pretended I had a boyfriend, Luke – who was really a girl called Lucy. Everyone found out and no one would talk to me. I got called names and stuff and left school for a while.

When I got back, nothing had changed, so I decided I would have to be strong and do it myself. I treated them as if they were stupid and just laughed at them. I made friends with some people who hadn't been very popular before. One boy even came out to me but said he wasn't going to tell anyone else because he saw what had happened to me. But we joked around and school became a laugh.

My mum and dad are great. I think my family might be unusual. Three of my friends have had really bad times, like one boy, his stepdad beat him up and kicked him out. Another girlfriend got thrown out, and my friend Denise… Well, when her mother heard about her girlfriend, she went straight to school and got the school to agree to put Denise and her friend in separate classes. She threatened to kill Denise and beat her really badly on her collarbone. She's petrified and really messed up. She used to come round to my house to feel safe.

Every Saturday and Tuesday I went to the Lesbian and Gay Youth Support Project in Manchester. This was for people between 14 and 24 but once a young boy who was 12 came along with his mum. We did games and made a float for Mardi Gras [lesbian and gay Pride] – and my mum and dad and sister Gina came to Mardi Gras. On Saturdays we had a study club where we got extra help with maths and stuff. We wrote a comedy called *Jayne's Revenge* about bullying and performed in theatres and community centres all over Manchester and Wigan; and we also toured in Ireland where we worked with a gay youth group in Dublin. It was really positive and good fun.

When I did my GCSE drama at school I said I wanted to write a play about a gay girl who gets bullied at school. She dies in the end. The drama teacher was really racist and homophobic and tried to stop me using the word gay. She said I might get bad marks from the examiner. But my group said OK, they would do it, and we performed it to the whole school including the bullies.

I was the gay girl and at one point I had to jump up and shout out I AM GAY! To my amazement, everyone cheered and clapped. They said they didn't realise I was really gay before. Since I left, lots of people I knew at school have come out to me but were too scared to do it at school.

The examiner really loved it. He said no one had ever done anything like it before and it was great. I got an A and the others all got good marks.

But the best thing ever was once I was in Lancaster in a shop and a girl came up to me and said, "You have made my life brilliant. You are my idol," and other stuff like that. She said she had seen me on TV and been through bad experiences at school. I said to her, "You have to have strength. I have been there. I know what it's like."

Alis Roberts is 17 and lives in Leigh, Lancashire. She is studying for her A-levels and hopes to travel next year and then go to art college. Her sister Gina wrote the next story, and then you can read what their dad has to say about having two gay daughters

Gina **refused** to give up when prejudice got in the way of her plans to set up a group at her college

Taking the lead

I had a very easy time coming out at 15. My family and friends were fine about it. But I was still in a very straight world. At seventeen I found out about Lesbian and Gay Youth Manchester, still an hour away but close enough to go there regularly.

It was great, suddenly finding myself with people who understood exactly the kinds of things I was feeling; and it was incredibly supportive, building up friendships with other young gay people. I realised how important it is for young gay and bisexual people to be able to find each other for support, friendship, and fun of course.

Then I found myself at college in Leigh, Lancashire. I was very 'out' there and other students would talk to me about their own sexuality. It soon became clear that although I could get away to Manchester there was a need for something more local. I asked the head of my college about setting up a lesbian and gay group. She promptly quoted Section 28 and said No Way. She was also concerned that as the age of consent for gay men was 18 (it's 16 for girls including lesbians) the college would get into trouble for allowing them to get together on the premises. As if we were going to set up a sex club in the lecture theatre! She could not be persuaded and the idea was dropped.

I got in touch with Leigh Well Women Centre. They said that if I did their training in counselling and safe sex and how to run the group, I could go ahead. They had a women-only policy so it could only be for lesbian and bisexual girls. In January 1997 Leigh Young Lesbian Group opened its doors.

The group ran for ten months, every week. From one to 12 young women came along and we'd talk, make things, write, play games, drink gallons of tea and coffee and just be together. The youth service was supportive and gave us

fight predjudice

money to buy books, so we had a mini library too.

In November I went travelling. There was no one to take over the group so it closed. When I returned, with an Australian girlfriend in tow, I moved to Sunderland to do a design degree at university. As far as I am aware there is still no group in Leigh. My 17-year-old sister, Alis, who is also lesbian, is now at the same college. She survived homophobic bullying at school and is now very politically active against Section 28. The college still won't have an LGB group but it is a relatively prejudice-free zone.

Gina Roberts is 21. She has contributed to the design and illustration of this book

Father of two

* Tony and Trixie Roberts are the parents of Gina and Alis, whose stories you've just read. Alis lives at home with them in Lancashire; Gina has left home. Jane Hoy asked Tony about his relationship with his daughters

Tony: It's hard to know what to say. No problem I suppose. I watched my daughters grow up and it sort of emerged. You see them with their friends, boys and girls, but their really deep relationships were with girls. Their relationships have been substantial, deep. They approach people openly – with no badges. That really pleases me.

Jane: Do you think your views are unusual?

Tony: I'm simply me. I suppose I'm liberal. I do know other people who think like me. I know a gay girl whose father is a vicar and it's not a problem. But if you are asking about our family, I think we share an interest in what people think and why, which is fascinating. The kids have grown up doing a lot of talking. Trixie and I talk. We like talking so things are out in the open. But judging from what other people say, they clearly have problems with different sexualities.

Really the thing in my life I have found most painful and difficult was that my older brother, well he's now my sister, changed sex. The children were eight and 12 when it happened so I suppose they grew up with it but I found it hurt. I felt threatened. When my brother decided he was a woman, I thought, if he can change, perhaps I am not what I thought I was – heterosexual that is. When we are talking now and I feel relaxed I sometimes slip into old ways and forget and say 'he' instead of 'she'. But my daughters' sense of freedom about themselves is no threat to me.

Jane: How did you react to Gina and Alis's experiences as they grew up?

Tony: Things happened in very different ways for each of them. Gina had to work it out on her own. Alis had Gina for an example and was more open about herself at school. But she made herself vulnerable. One day she wrote a poem of sympathy to a girl who had just lost her boyfriend. Some girls who had been bullying her snatched the poem and fights broke out. Alis refused to go back to school, she was so upset. I was very angry at the school. I must say part of me was cross with my daughter too. I thought she shouldn't get so upset, should stand up for herself like I imagined I would do. But I was far more cross with the teacher. The headmistress implied that Alis should hide her sexuality because of the problems it gave the school and her teacher virtually said 'what do you expect if you write things like that'. Well it was just a poem between two friends, hardly a love poem or anything.

Jane: What advice have you for parents who have daughters who are questioning their sexuality?

Tony: Focus on the person who is growing inside. A young person is fascinating. Who they prefer to spend time with. What they think. What they read. What they do with their day. Their gender and sexuality is important but it's only one of those things that make up that person. And spend time talking about everything. Youth support groups are useful. We used to drive Alis to Manchester to the lesbian and gay support group and it certainly helped her to come to terms with herself. Manchester also has an association for families of gay children and although I don't feel the

My daughter

⁎Linda Deakin talks about her relationship with her lesbian daughter – and her gay son!

When I was pregnant, I had all the usual anxieties. I worried that my child might not be healthy, that he or she might not be as intelligent as others at school. I hoped the child would be attractive to look at and might have some special talents. I never gave a thought to the sexuality of that child.

Twenty-three years ago, I gave birth to a daughter, and my fears were unfounded. As she grew, it became apparent that she would be pretty, above average intelligence and her health was excellent. Even better, she was a talented artist. Everyone commented on her boyish behaviour. She hated wearing anything girlie and had her lovely long hair cut off a few days after starting school. Then came the football with the boys in the street. As a teenager, she joined a girls' team – and there was a definite lack of interest in male pop stars and actors. Still, that would come in time. She was just a tomboy, that was all. Anyway, I was too wrapped up in my feelings about my son, 14 months younger and obviously (to me at least) gay from nursery-school age.

Girls can be tomboys, they can wear trousers and cut their hair. It's different with boys. A little boy who loves dolls and cuddly toys when he is 12, enjoys drama and dancing, has no male friends and sits in his bedroom giggling with a bunch of girls instead of watching football or motor sport on TV… add to that the fact that he's really quite camp, and he just *has* to be gay.

By the time they were both in their late teens, I thought I knew my children. My son was gay. I knew for sure when he was 17 and visited gay clubs quite openly. His father knew too, didn't much like it but accepted that the son who would never go with him to the match or stand at the bar having a pint with him was not a bad lad. After all, his sexuality was only a part of him.

Shortly after her 18th birthday, my daughter drank a bottle of wine, sat beside me on the sofa and told me she was gay too. "Oh," I said, "you're not, are you?"

"Yes – didn't you know?" I felt so guilty. I hadn't known, I never picked up on it and somehow, I felt I should. I couldn't believe it. Not her too. Not *both* of them! Was it me? Did I eat something when I was pregnant? Or was it the football her father bought her when she was 15? Those are the kind of stupid questions I asked myself. Me! I thought I knew so much about gay people. I had no problems with them and knew a few. I had made a point of reading about HIV and other stuff because of my son, but I suddenly realised I knew very little about lesbians.

It took a while to come to terms with having two gay offspring. But I did it. Some members of the family have not been told and there is no need to tell them. I'm very proud of my children and I put up with the comments from the sad homophobes out there unless they say something so horrible and stupid that I just *have* to speak.

My two are 'out' to most but not everyone. My son is out at work but my daughter isn't, so I have to respect that and carefully choose the people I tell. I listen to the usual stupidity. I mean, everyone thinks they know what gay men 'do'. But when they know about my daughter, they often ask me what her and her partner do in bed. I always answer with, "I've no idea, do you ask your children what they do?"

My brother-in-law believes that all a lesbian needs is a good bloke to 'change her'. My hairdresser reckons that I'm cursed by something my parents did and that's why I have two gay children. Oh well!

I still feel isolated at times. If there's a problem, I'd love to talk about it to the next-door neighbour over coffee, but I can't. Not if it's about a problem with one of their partners or something like that.

Only the other week I got over another hurdle. My daughter and her partner proved that they trust me. I was visiting their house and they sat opposite me on the sofa. While talking, my daughter's partner put her arm across the back of the sofa and as she did so, she stroked my daughter's face lovingly. I smiled at them, it seemed so natural. Two women who were in love, best friends, soulmates, demonstrating the love and mutual respect they have for each other with a soft, gentle caress.

It was several minutes before I realised that it was the first time they had done that and the first time I had felt 'comfortable'. I don't feel I have a 'lesbian' daughter these days, I just have a daughter. A picture of her, arm in arm with her partner, sits proudly on the dressing table – although I haven't brought it downstairs yet, as much for their sake as ours.

Now for the next hurdle: watching the same thing with my son! I love my children and they are simply two young people starting out in life. It's been a long time since I wished they were straight. The last time was the Soho bombings when I realised there were people out there who wished my children dead. I hope this doesn't happen again.

Linda Deakin lives near Wolverhampton and is a volunteer for Parents' Friend, which offers a listening ear to parents who think one (or more) of their offspring might be gay. See the Info zone for details

Dear Grandma Doris

I guess I just don't know how to start…

Grandma, I know that you can hear this and I know in my heart that you'll always love me, but there were things I wanted to tell you. How could I, though? How could I tell my greatgrandma I was gay? I wanted to, believe me I did, Grandma, but the words never came and the time was never right.

And now it's too late. I was coming to see you when we found out you had died.

You weren't ever supposed to die – you were 98 and going strong. You were going to celebrate your 100th birthday with me. We were going to get a letter from the Queen… But it's gone, you're gone. I miss you.

I wonder how you would react. I know you wouldn't have been cross – you would probably have said something like "whatever makes you happy" – but I wanted to show you. I wanted you to meet my girlfriend. I wanted to tell you I was finally happy. But I couldn't. My mum doesn't accept it, my nana doesn't accept it, why should you?

But you were always different – always doing things differently. You would never be told what to do. You married a man your family wasn't keen on, but you loved him and that was what mattered. I love Su and that's what matters, right? But if love is all that matters, why couldn't my parents stand to look at me? And why did I feel so hated when my only confession was that I was in love?

I wish I could hold you once more. I wish you could squeeze my hand and tell me it's OK. But you can't. I'd like to have the chance to tell you, to give you the opportunity to tell me what you thought. You would have loved me no less. You loved us all. You would have told my mum not to fuss so much and that I was making myself happy.

I'm gay. It took me a long time to say that. I tortured myself for months on end about it. I couldn't be gay and I couldn't put my mum through her 'worst nightmare' by admitting it. I spent months debating all this inside my head, thinking about how things should be. I had boyfriends. Most of them were just a cover-up, just pretending.

It started with rumours at school, which Su told me about. She thought I was gay and was waiting for me to tell her. Seems weird how she knew. I finally told her and when we became closer we 'came out' as a couple at school. I wish we hadn't as it caused problems with some teachers. I'd told my close friends first and none of them were surprised. It seems everyone else knew before I did.

Mum and Dad reacted badly, but they soon began to deal with it. Although they never will want to know or understand, they are beginning to accept at least tolerating it. I knew what their reactions would be. Mum had already threatened me when I was younger. I used to joke about it and she'd always say how I must never do that to her. I don't think she understood I wasn't doing it to hurt her – I had to be honest with my own feelings and to all the people I loved.

But I wasn't being honest, because I didn't tell you the truth. You'd ask if I had any boyfriends – or gentleman friends, as you liked to call them. Mum would always look at me with tears in her eyes and I'd say, "No Grandma…"

You didn't want me to be something I wasn't, but when I told you I wasn't going into the RAF, the disappointment was clear. My whole family was proud that I was going to be an RAF Officer. But it was a dream so easily shattered by the fact that I wasn't allowed to join the RAF because of my sexuality. I couldn't tell you all the real reason. But I felt that the reason was just another sign that this was a bad thing. How could I be proud of being gay and being myself if I was suddenly made to feel like it was all so wrong?

I keep telling myself that I know you love me and I know you'd understand, but I can't see it anymore. I think it's because I can't see you and tell you face to face. I can't see you smile at me and hold my hand. Why can't I trust my judgement and believe you would have told me not to worry and not to be so scared? Why can't I find the answers?

I feel so afraid. Why, if I know all of this, do I feel like you wouldn't approve? Why was I putting my mother through all of this? To be honest I don't even think I know why I hurt my mum.

You know that less than two weeks after you died I took an overdose. The doctors said I was going to die. We hadn't even buried you. You came to me, you sat on my bed and waved your finger at me like I'd only stolen a bis-cuit, but you said that I couldn't leave Mum. I thought it was real and that you were alive. I just lay there in the hospital thinking about you visiting me, until I remembered.

I let you down that day. No matter what anyone says, I know that I let you down. I gave up. I surrendered. I let them all get to me. I'll never do it again, I know that now, but I can't cope with the pain of not knowing your response. I love you Grandma, and I wish that I had told you.

Love you forever, Sam xxx

My auntie is a lesbian

My mum drove me out of school one day and parked by the seafront and said, "Don't be upset, your auntie is a lesbian." I said, "What, Kate's a dyke?" Thinking YES! My mum had a fit at me for using "that kind of language". I was thrilled. I felt an instant connection. Ever since I came out (four years later) we've got on like a house on fire. I'll always have a special bond with her. She is my favourite relative. She is the best, always offering love, support and a shoulder when I need it.

Kate's niece

girl2girl

Out in the world

Coming out

I had my first sexual experience with a girl at eight years old. It was more experimenting. At the age of 12, her mum walked in and shit hit the fan. We were told to get dressed and go downstairs. My friend's mum kept us apart and my friend started dating boys. I was told never to tell anyone.

My mum was great, but asked me the weirdest questions. How do you have sex? I answered that as nicely as possible. My dad was annoyed and said he already knew. He still thinks it's just a phase. We both fight over Sandra Bullock and he says he thought he only had one son.

My brother was great and we get on a lot better than we used to. We have fights about who has the most gorgeous girl. My little sister really thought it was good to have a lezzie sister and buys me the most weirdest things. It makes me sad to think about it but she told a friend she trusted about me, and that friend told her class. She got picked on at school and one girl asked her if she was a lezzie which my little sister found very upsetting and confusing.

My best friend, she said the funniest things. We were having a smoke and I told her and she asked me if I fancied her. I said no, she wasn't my type, and she got upset wondering what was wrong with her! I told her nothing was wrong with her and explained to her who my ideal women were and then she understood. Then she asked me what kind of clothes lesbians wear and will I be changing my wardrobe. I laughed and told her I was not changing anything, I am staying me.

Lucy, 18, Yorkshire

Discovering myself

I've known I was gay since as far back as being nine years old in primary school. It was a scary thing to realise that instead of worrying about what games I was going to play at break or what sweets I was going to get after school, I found myself asking why I fancied the nursery school teacher, a woman! I kept those feelings hidden but when I got to secondary school I started asking questions and began the journey of discovering myself. I knew what I was and what it meant but I couldn't accept it.

I hated myself for being this way and couldn't understand what was happening to me. There were times I would cry myself to sleep and I even had thoughts of how I could make my problem go away in the least painful and quickest way. I couldn't tell anyone else what I was feeling because I couldn't say it to myself let alone anyone else. I would try and make myself attracted to men to see if I was 'normal' and to stop people asking questions.

There was this one lad at school, Ben, who all the girls fancied. He was funny, good looking and had a body like Peter André. Everyone wanted a piece. I told everyone I had a crush on him. I even convinced myself which was easy to do because there was no way he would go for someone like me. We became good friends and spent a lot of time with each other. I would even go so far as to say that I loved him. Not in a sexual way but as a friend.

I used to talk to my friends about gay people to see what their reactions would be and to try and work out what they would do if I told them I was gay. I even asked them, "What would you do if one of us said we were gay?" They all said it wouldn't make any difference. But I still wasn't confident.

It became more obvious that this was something that wasn't going to go away. As a result it became harder for me to hide. I would spend all my spare time doing things. I was in a band with Ben, did voluntary work and sport. This helped when people asked why I hadn't got a boyfriend. I was too busy.

More coming out stories

Here are some of our contributors talking about what happened to them

....

Dee: One of my friends came out to me and I'd been thinking for about a year that I might be gay. I told him and we've been best friends ever since. If I hadn't met him I honestly don't think I would have admitted it to myself. We've been through everything. Our first trip to the [Manchester gay] village together. First partners, more partners, more nights out. It made me feel free and invincible to be out and proud. Of sorts! Then I came out to my best friend up the road and she said she always knew and to give her the gossip.

....

Reena: It's going to be quite life changing to come out to all of my family. My mum knows as she's most important. My mum and twin sister and me, we're close like sisters. My best friend lives four doors away and all my grandparents live within 20 minutes. I'm friends with my aunt and uncle, cousins, mum's friends and godparents.

More coming out stories

Sue D: I came out to one of my best friends when I was 15 because I needed to tell someone how happy I was that I fancied a Spice Girl. She was more traumatised by the fact that it was a Spice Girl than that it was a woman, especially because she said Baby Spice looked like a hamster and therefore I had bad taste. With my mum, I said, "You know me and Sam are..." and she said, "Good friends?" in a knowing kind of way. I replied, "Well her parents have found out and are on their way to kill me." I think she took it well.

Sarah: I was outed to my mum and friends by a girl I was in love with. Her mum found a letter I wrote and phoned my mum. She said it was just a phase. I was terrified. I couldn't face my mum and my sister. It was embarrassing.

Shani: I come out to everyone all the time.

One day in school Ben asked me out in front of all my mates. I said yes. Maybe it would work. After a few days I realised it wouldn't, though I did want it to as we had a lot in common.

When I got to college I carried on spending all my spare time with the band. Ben was the first person I told how I was feeling. I just couldn't deal with it on my own anymore. I had done it for nine years. We went into the kitchen and I said, "Ben I need to tell you something. I'm gay and I'm so scared." Then I broke down. He held me in his arms for about half an hour. It was one of the most powerful experiences I've ever had. Ben was very accepting and it took some of the pressure off me.

Not long after, I was told that two of the female members of the band were dating. I was gutted because I had a crush on one of them but had never said anything because I thought she was straight. They would go to a gay pub in town and I would go along with them. I used to say, "I don't mind coming to gay pubs. It's not like I have a problem with it. Anyway the atmosphere is better." Eventually I admitted I was gay. It was a great weight off my shoulders but now I lived in fear that they would tell my other friends and everyone would find out. Worst of all, my family and parents would find out. I still wasn't comfortable with myself and wanted to be 'normal'.

I left college and on my first day at work my 15-year-old brother was killed by a drunk driver. In that instant my world fell apart. As a result I became a new person. I realised life's too short. If you can't be who you are and go out there and get what you want, then what's the point? The day we stop resisting our instincts, we will have learned to live. This helped me accept myself.

I met my first girlfriend at work. She was ten years older than me with two kids, though they didn't live with her. She guessed I was gay and before long we were having heart to hearts and spending loads of time together, though only as friends. I just remember feeling happy because for once I was being myself. Before long rumours were going round work and we both denied everything.

After a few months we split. As a result I became best friends with her flatmate. She taught me to be happy with who I was. She made me accept I was gay and gave me so much support and confidence. I will forever be grateful to her and love her with all my heart.

Soon after, I went to Ireland as a volunteer. My confidence showed and before too long friends were finding out. But when they asked me, I just said yes. A few friends saw this as an experiment, using me. It's like I had become this magnet to 'wannabes'. I'm constantly getting female friends telling me they have developed strong feelings for me and are even in love with me. I want to be genuine with one of these friends for whom I have growing feelings, but deep down I know she is just curious and I'm an ideal candidate for her.

Now I'm living in a community with 11 other volunteers. I recently told them all. It's great. After months of talking to them about people I like and exes, without ever mentioning a name, saying 'they' 'them' and 'this person', I don't have to watch what I say anymore. The hardest was telling my roommate. What if she freaked out?

I just said, "Do you want to see a photo of my ex?"

"Oh yes, the guy back home?"

"Not really." I showed her the photo of me and another woman.

"Oh... er, are you gay?"

"Yes Kathryn, I am. Are you OK with sharing a room and all?"

"Yes, it's not like you are going to pounce on me in the middle of the night. You are still you."

Now we are closer than ever and it's great. The fact that I have Mel C all over the bedroom walls makes sense to her now. After ten years I no longer have to live a double life.

The hardest thing is keeping it from my family and most of all from my mum. It's easier to tell friends. If they don't like it, you can push them aside and find new ones. You can't do that with family. They can't be replaced. I don't want to be a disappointment to them and I don't want them to look at me differently. That they will reject me is what scares me most.

Jen Ashton is 19. She was brought up in Sheffield. At college she studied for the police force, coached her own basketball team and ran play schemes. She is now a volunteer at Corrymeela, a reconciliation centre in Northern Ireland

More coming out stories

Sam: I came out to everyone. I was so delighted to put a name to all the feelings inside me. I was happy to tell people. Everyone was great and very supportive. Some said they always knew I was gay before I did. I cried and laughed with relief. My brother said, "So that's why you watched *Ellen*!"

....

Kate: I told my mum I was bisexual on Boxing Day 1995. I said, "Mum, I've got something to tell you." (What a cliché!) She said, "You're pregnant!" (Inward groan.)

....

Liz: I blurted out to my mum while I was doing the washing up. She thought it best to tell my dad. She cried and didn't understand because I had fancied men. She cried some more and then hugged me and told me she loved me.

3 words

i am gay

Three words,
Them three words
At first I didn't understand their meaning
And then I pretended to.

I can't believe it,
You said them three words
You've changed my life,
I mean, you can't.

How can this be?
Surely you're confused?
Oh my god what have I done?
I brought you to this world.

How can you say it?
Have you no shame?
Them three words.
'I am gay.'
Mother, I said those three words
And now you know
My life, a masquerade played
For you.

I am (me)
Happy
Proud &
Free

Do three words really change things?
I'm still me.
The child you bore,
The child you loved.

Can this bond be so easily broken?
By three, simple, words,
Mother,
'I am gay.'

Joni, 18, wrote this poem when she was 15. She lives with her family in east London where she was brought up

Nasty comments

I feel threatened by homophobia
It causes claustrophobia

Homophobic bullies keep us in the closet
Just hold up your head and tell them to sod it

Nasty comments cause great harm
These kind of people belong in a farm.

Sara, 19, lives in Bradford

Bullied at school

I was bullied at school, not for being a lesbian. Cripple, cripple, they would shout. I was in so much pain. The names didn't compare to the physical pain I had to tolerate. I have muscular dystrophy. I've been waiting four years for an electric wheelchair and five years for operations. Life has been hell at times. Then the question of my sexuality came about. Deep down inside I knew really that I was a lesbian. I didn't have much choice. Having an illness and being a lesbian, it's just the way I am.

There was a boy in school. Cripple, cripple, cripple! he would shout. Looking back, he must have been in a lot of pain. I guess he must have hated me cos he could see himself in me. I hated him in school.

I hadn't seen him in years, then I bumped into him and he asked me out for a drink. I went. We went to a gay bar. Chris, he is called. Chris, he is my lifeline. I lived with foster carers, some good, some bad. It didn't really work out. I moved into a flat with Chris.

I went through a bad phase a year ago. I was in constant pain. I had Chris looking after my pills and me. All I wanted was comfort. The doctors, they just don't seem to understand, and I can't get through to them. The waiting list looked like as long as a lifetime. I could not wait that long. I was in such pain, I couldn't handle it anymore, I just wanted to be normal, and I didn't want to feel ill anymore. I took my pills. All of them, just to take the pain away and be done with it.

I'm so glad my friends found me. We do have a laugh. And Chris, where would he be without me? He pushes my chair everywhere. I'm still waiting for an electric one. And my operation. But I think one day it will be all right.

I have good days and I have bad days, you've got to hang on to what you've got and look at the good aspects of life. If I feel that desperate now, I phone a friend and they come round. I'm so glad my friends found me.

Lorraine, 18, Avon

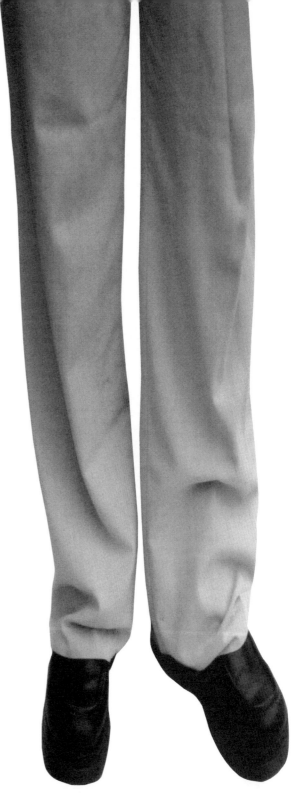

Homophobia

Am I mental and dirty?
People say I'm a bit flirty.

I feel freaked at people who are violent
It scares me so I feel silent

It's verbal abuse to call someone queer
When this happens I feel like a beer

I get pissed off when I get hate mail
People who send it should go to jail

I think bigots are so small
I stand so proud I feel so tall.

Sara, 19, lives in Bradford

LOOK OUT FOR NUMBER ONE

Not the Only Fruit
(a young lesbian group at Phase, East London) say:

- *Be yourself* • *Ignore prejudice and discrimination*
- *Use all resources available to you* • *Give as good as you get*
- *Be an individual, don't be led* • *Learn from other people's mistakes or your own –*
  whichever come first! • *Let people presume!*
- *Don't let your parents find out from someone else: it's always*
  better coming from you. Pick your moment carefully.

Despised

When so many can despise you
By only knowing your name
It makes you sit and wonder
And put your life into frame

When you're guilty of nothing but being yourself
And everyone has something to say
Do you look forward and face them
Or turn and walk away?

When your name has been changed
To something you have never been
I'm guilty of one and only one crime
If living my life is a sin

When you have hurt no one but yourself
And everyone's out to get you
You wonder if being you is a problem
Should you be someone new?

But then how can you be anything
Than the person you really are?
If you are pressured to be someone else
Your life will be behind bars

So to anyone that despises me
There's only one thing to say:
This is me so deal with it
I cannot be any other way

Jodie Kearley works as an administrator
in Brighton, Sussex. She is out at work

More coming out stories

Mel: When I explained I'm bisexual, my mum just sat, head in her hands, not looking at me. She didn't say anything for ages until I said, "Aren't you going to say something?" She asked me if I was seeing someone and when she found out it was a man, she said, "So why did you have to tell me then?"
After arguing that it was because I might have a girlfriend one day, and her not understanding it, I walked out in a huff. I was really angry and didn't talk to her for months. She still won't accept me and in a recent letter said I wasn't bisexual and blamed my dad for making me think I'm a man. (Hmm, don't think so!) I haven't told my dad – we don't talk – but I know it would be his worst nightmare.

Ruth: Like mother like daughter. I came out to my mother at 14. Two years later she's a lesbian! There's a few things I need to teach her. She's not quite got the grasp. My best friends thought it was cool and asked lots of questions.

More coming out stories

Carly: My mum, sister and all my friends were fantastic. In fact everyone seemed to know I was gay before I did. I haven't told anyone else in the family as I think their religious beliefs will affect their reaction. My grandparents are of the condemning generation. In fact when I introduced them to one of my openly gay male friends, my grandad had a huge debate about it [homosexuality] being 'unclean'.

....

Julia: My mum's supported me by telling me that she's proud of me no matter what. She even lets my girlfriend stay at my house. She says its's taken a bit of time for her to get used to seeing me with my girl-friend, but we don't shove it in her face. She has helped me through a few lovers' tiffs and things as well.

....

Cassie: I asked my dad if he had ever considered sleeping with a man. He said no. I said, "Well neither have I."

What being a lesbian means to me

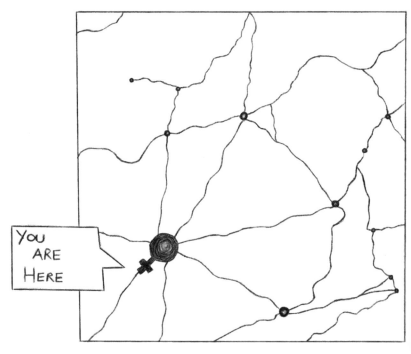

Julia Collar

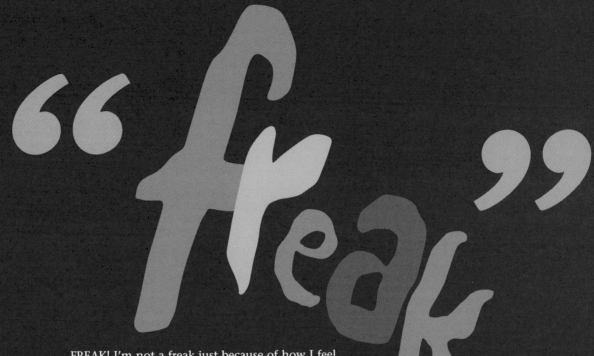

FREAK! I'm not a freak just because of how I feel
You should not judge me, these
feelings I have are real!
You shouldn't think I fancy you, our
friendship's not that way,
Understand that pervert is *not* another
word for gay!
If you believe in love, then anything
can happen to you,
It doesn't matter the age, sex or race,
it can still be true!
Please accept what I am, and maybe
you will see,
No matter who I love,
I will always be
me!

Emma, 21

Phase fightback

Tracy, Adele, Layla, Sarah and Fiona are aged 16-23 and members of Not the Only Fruit, a lesbian group at Phase, a youth project in east London. They wrote these poems with other young gay people for a project for World Aids Day 1999, planned to highlight the lives of young people and children affected by HIV and AIDS. They were invited to read their poems at the event.

But at the last minute, the organisers of the event decided that having poetry read by lesbian and gay young people was too controversial. Using Section 28 as an excuse, they banned the group from reading their work – they said the reading could be seen as 'promoting homosexuality' (see 'Words' in Info zone for details of Section 28).

Everyone felt disappointed, angry and silenced. They wrote to the organisers asking for reasons. They didn't get a reply.

Phase is now working on a peer education project. Young people will go into schools and colleges to do workshops about homophobia, sexual health and HIV. They're working hard to support each other, and to challenge the way people in authority often use Section 28 to back up their prejudices.

Meanwhile, here are three of the 'banned' poems, for all the world to see!

Vaccination

Information on television
People's views
Pamphlets, books, slots on the news
Deadly disease
Finding a cure
Combination therapies
People unsure
Hope in research
A vital vaccine
So AIDS is not heard of
So AIDS is not seen

Isolation

I am here
All alone
Feel like crying
How did it happen
All so fast
All too quickly

Only human

I realise that I could die
Not understanding how or why
That being straight or gay
All I know could be taken away
That prejudice causes so much fear
Wish all the hate would disappear
Realising it could happen to me
That no one has immunity
AIDS seems so final
There is yet no cure
People confused, people unsure
Being only human we tend to try
To run away, not understand why
This illness does not pick and choose
But everyone tends to lose

See Info zone for information about HIV and AIDS

Wake up, we're

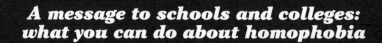

A message to schools and colleges: what you can do about homophobia

- Zero tolerance of homophobic and anti-gay behaviour
- Make it clear that discrimination is not accepted
- Clamp down on homophobic behaviour
- All sex education classes should contain all aspects of sexuality
- Display leaflets and information
- Have a group where people can feel safe and welcome
- Start supporting us
- Offer counselling
- Make being gay not such a big deal, then homophobia would be less
- Section 28 should be abolished. We are all equal, treat us all the same!
- There are no official constraints with the clause – gay issues can be conveyed legally
- Sex awareness classes for gays and lesbians
- Lesbian and gay societies
- Awareness weeks
- More gay role models, whether in school or literature
- Recruit women and lesbian healthcare officials to educate students
- Introduce more literature about lesbian and gay relationships and lifestyles
- Encourage open discussions about issues
- Generally make people feel comfortable with who they are
- Value lesbian and gay contributions to your studies and society
- Have gay and lesbian speakers in to talk about their lives
- Discuss ways that gay couples can become parents
- Help lesbian/gay/bisexual students prepare themselves for the homophobia they face when they get a job

From the contributors to girl2girl

n the year 2000!

Youth worker's view

Everyone who works in education has a 'duty of care' and this should extend to all young people. Some teachers seem to have 'chosen' to be unclear about what Section 28 actually allows them to do – whether giving information or discussing homosexuality is *promotion*, and therefore contravenes Section 28. So young lesbians, gays or bisexuals can feel isolated with little or no emotional support – and homophobic bullying can remain unreported and unchallenged.

Youth workers in lesbian, gay and bisexual youth projects are very aware of the implications of Section 28 and work within it. We are able to provide positive role models (through staff, media images and information) and the peer support which is not available in schools and colleges in the UK. In some ways we have to work harder to improve a young person's self-image and self-esteem which formal education has failed to do. The main thing that a lesbian, gay and bisexual youth project *will* promote is self-empowerment and positive feelings in a safe environment.

Julia Tipton, youth worker with Not the Only Fruit at Phase

Scrap the Section!

"Section 28 is ridiculous. It stops gay teenagers really getting the help they need and it stops teachers thinking they can challenge people who are homophobic and stop bullying. I don't think you could make a child gay by promoting homosexuality even if you wanted to. Lots of children discover they are gay even when they're brought up in a very heterosexual environment at school and home. I think children should be taught about homosexuality as part of sex education and it should be made clear it is an acceptable relationship."

Sarah, 18

girl2girl

Living the life

*Village life

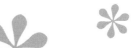

I have known about my sexuality all my life. I can still remember having a crush on Kylie Minogue when she was in *Neighbours* over ten years ago. My mum used to call me downstairs when she was on TV. Back then I never quite understood. It was something I just didn't want to deal with. At 14 my thoughts and feelings became too strong and I decided to come to terms with how I felt. Depression was causing me to lose sleep and put on weight.

It wasn't easy going through school with a deep dark secret. Homophobia was a main theme for most of my life at Melton Comprehensive. There was a girl in my class who looked butch and had short cropped hair, so for those reasons and those reasons alone she was constantly bullied. One by one her friends turned against her until there was no one left to support and defend her.

There was no way I wanted to live with that kind of pressure and torment so I too joined in with these accusations so they didn't suspect me. I carry the guilt of that decision to this day. She is now preparing for university and is in a long-term relationship with a man who loves and respects her. I don't blame her if she never forgave me for what I did. I of all people should have known better. She was a good friend and I threw it all back in her face.

Now I'm the subject of torment. Though 90% of those I have told have been brilliant, there are still a few people who hate me for who I am.

In my first year of college, I made friends with a girl whose advice, love and support will remain with me for the rest of my life. Ursula was the first person I trusted enough to tell about my sexuality. She introduced me to her gay friends, which helped me not to feel so alienated. Slowly but surely I built enough trust with other students who I could tell, and soon I had a small community of friends I felt comfortable with.

I could never have told my friends in the tiny village in which I live. They've known me my whole life and I could not face rejection from those closest to me, especially as my area thrives on rumours. Living in a goldfish bowl, the shit floats around until it sticks to something, and I couldn't take the risk of my homophobic family finding out.

It was around this time that I met Henry. He had moved back to the village to spend time with his parents who he hadn't seen in five years. We became good friends, and I considered telling him on several occasions but never had enough guts to do so.

Then one day his sister came down from London for the week. We all went to our local for a drink and she mentioned quietly to me that she was gay. I didn't know quite how to react. It made me a bit nervous as Anne is very attractive and I didn't want to make it too obvious that I liked her, so I just said, "Oh really, so am I."

The next day she came round to see me. I'd never really fancied anyone I knew before, just movie and rock stars, so my heart was racing when she was actually sat in my room talking to me. We saw a lot of each other before she returned to London, and on the last day of her visit I told her how I felt. I was so nervous. She told me she felt the same, though at the time I didn't believe her.

I will never forget the moment I realised that I was falling in love. We were at a nightclub for a friend's birthday. I was on the dance floor with my mate Rich and as I looked up to the balcony where Anne was stood chatting, the neon lights passed over her soft white skin, making her dress and hair light up and look as if she were made of porcelain and gold. At that moment she smiled down at me and filled me with a feeling I haven't managed to shake off since.

We went home that night and made love for the first time. It was truly amazing. I was nervous but excited in the same breath. The anticipation of her smooth touch was incredible. I have never been so happy in all my life. Next morning I couldn't believe that I was next to her, her arm gently gripping my waist as she was sleeping. I lay there silent with a smile which lasted until we had to say goodbye again.

I went to London as often as I could to see her and she came down with her six-year-old daughter Megan in the holidays. But it was still hard being so far apart. The age gap between us is 12 years but it has never really been a problem. Her family accept me and Henry has been great. But it was our friends that worried me most. I didn't know how Anne's friends would take me or if their relationship with Anne would change. I didn't want them to think badly of me as I am younger.

On her next visit Anne told a mutual friend of our relationship, who then proceeded to tell others and spread rumours about the village. This soon turned my blissful existence into a nightmare. For weeks I got hurtful looks and some outrageous accusations. I couldn't handle my best friend Elaine or my parents finding out about my love for Anne, as I was certain they wouldn't understand.

But I was wrong about Elaine. When I finally had enough courage to tell her she was great but she just couldn't understand why I had never said anything before. We had always shared everything and never had any secrets, though it was as if I was a liar and our friendship would never be complete due to my secret. With her support I set the record straight.

It was hard but I had the love and help from six special people, Anne, Elaine, Henry, Ursula, Rich and Charlie. Charlie was another good friend who stuck up for me on several occasions when people were putting me down. Once he even knocked down a guy who was giving me grief. It's at times like these you find out who your true friends are.

My parents still don't know about my sexuality. It makes it even harder now that Anne works part-time for my mum and they have some kind of a friendship. I'm surprised they haven't found out through the grapevine. Though I wouldn't know what to say if they did. I don't think Anne understands how hard it is for me, as her family are so accepting of her sexuality and mine wouldn't have a clue.

I guess it is one of the biggest regrets that I have. I know my family love me but for how long? I'm sure that it would change things and all I want is to make them happy and I can't do that in the way they want me to. I'm tired of living this lie but I need them. I'm only 18 and I know that I can't make it out there on my own. I do plan telling them in the future but not until I've got through college and I'm standing on my own two feet.

Jez, 18, lives in a small Dorset village and studies photography

*It's odd being a dyke

It's odd being a dyke in this day and age. People assume it's easy, especially older lesbians. It's not. As an 18-year-old lesbian, I can honestly say that I have been there and done that. I was a member of a rugby team so I had obviously slept with half of them before I told my mates. They all knew already and were really great. That's the easy bit.

My parents were a different kettle of fish. I was close to my mum but not really to my dad. So I guess it hurt Mum more. Imagine a middle-aged woman who is rather prim and proper standing up and calling her daughter a "fucking pervert" before walking out of the room.

My dad stood up and said it didn't matter, he still loved me and as long as I was happy, so was he. That hug was one of the best moments of my life. Now my mum is getting used to it. She even asks about my girlfriends. My sister had already figured it out and was really great. My brother suddenly became very amusing. I'll never forget the way he asked me if I used strap-ons.

My first shag with a woman was shit. I mean, I lay there trembling nervously while a mate went down on me. All I could think of was the fact that I hadn't showered that day. But I had slept with men when I was younger and that wasn't exactly awe-inspiring either! Now I can honestly say I am a sex goddess. I've worked at it with my current girlfriend and learnt to communicate. It causes blushes. Trust me, I know. But once you've started you can't stop. I know it's a cliché but a damn good one.

I came out at school when I was 17. It got me a lot of attention. I came out at my school leavers' ball. It was great. There I was, all dressed up in a wonderful silver dress, long velvet gloves and a fancy hairdo. I just walked up to make a speech of thanks to the teachers and everything tumbled out of my mouth. I got a standing ovation. I couldn't believe how easy it was or how great I felt.

I'm not saying do the same as I did cos you've gotta remember: Be careful. I didn't, and I ended up getting raped by two of the lads in my year. They seemed convinced that all I needed was a good hard dicking. Oh how wrong they were!

I survived. Got over it and came to Uni, the place where I believed life would be easy. How wrong can a person get? I'm living in halls and it's hard. I went from school where most of the lads were fine and had a joke with me. Even my bro could call me a rug-muncher without offence and the girls were intrigued by my sexuality. I had slept with a few of them. In halls of residence, lads have big problems. Some still won't speak to me even after four months. I have got into fights with some and been called every name under the sun by others. But I have my good friends, both gay and straight, to help me through it. You just gotta remember that not everyone is scared of difference.

I'm still here at Uni and having the time of my life. Brighton's great. It's not a certainty that you'll pull, but I always manage it so it can't be that hard. I'm in a great relationship and v.v.v. happy. If people have a problem with you, it's their problem, not yours. Let them deal with it. I try.

Laura Sheppard, 18, is from Nottingham. She is now a student at the University of Brighton

*Here's me!

I'm a 20-year-old gay girl who has been 'out' now almost five years. Coming out was the best thing I ever did. I am completely honest about who I am and as I'm open it attracts like-minded people, which is exactly what I always hoped for.

Just like Nathan in *Queer as Folk*, I came out when I was still at school but I certainly didn't 'explode' out of the closet. So far it has taken five years. It is an ongoing process. New situations arise when you have to tell new people so unless you are stereotypically gay and obvious you are never completely out.

I never held any parties in honour of my coming out and no one congratulated me on being gay, which is what I had hoped would happen! The first milestone in my coming out has to be when I came out to my diary, which was ultimately myself. I was 16 and there were some mild fireworks in my head. I finally had a way of venting my confusion and discussing girls I liked. It was great and made me feel like I was speaking to someone. I filled the entire diary within two months. I had so much to say and could say it without fear of reprisals. I would definitely recommend keeping a diary to anyone trying to come to terms with their sexuality. It puts things in perspective without you even realising it. I think the opening phrase of that entry was, "Tonight, Matthew, I'm going to be a dyke. Oh yeah, and every other night too." Alongside was a picture of Beth Jordache I had slyly torn out of a friend's teen magazine.

Beth Jordache was my heroine but by that time she had been killed off. I had cried at such an injustice. I felt I knew her and when she died I felt really lost. I found it hard to distinguish between television and reality when Beth was in *Brookside* because I wanted her to be real. It was my only concrete evidence that there were others like me out there. I had not met any other gay people and religiously wrote to various organisations looking for penpals and ways of meeting other people.

My first real personal contact with gay people came about from the Aberdeen Lesbian Gay and Bisexual Society at the university. I had made an appointment with people who'd set up a 16 and under youth group, every second Saturday. I found it really beneficial to know that there was someone there if I needed them. It also gave me a break away from my 'other life' where no one knew I was gay. Away from all the lies I had to tell and the pretences I had to live under.

I don't really regret not having told any of my friends at that point as it gave me a kind of buzz, sneaking around doing things, going places that they would never have expected. I knew I had to wait until the time was right for me before I told them.

It took me at least six months before I decided the time was just right. Even then I initially only told one person – my best male friend. I couldn't have hoped for a better reaction from him. He didn't care and together we conquered Aberdeen's gay scene, all one club of it. There were so many gay people! I couldn't imagine where they all came from. It was certainly an eye-opener.

Throughout school I continued to come out to more and more people, all of whom were very supportive and did not look at me any different than they had before. In fact, peer-wise, I think I have been very lucky and have yet to have a bad experience. Perhaps that's why I never felt right about telling my story – because I have no negative experiences for others to relate to. But there have to be some positive stories so people know that there is hope for them not to receive any negativity. I never received any form of homophobic abuse at school. This is surprising considering that the statistics of those who do is worryingly high. Even one of my teachers knew, through an essay I had written as part of my Higher English. She was fantastic about it, although I don't think I have seen her since a Freudian slip on the last day of term resulted in me telling her I fancied her!

I wouldn't say that I was the 'school dyke' but as far as I'm aware it was pretty common knowledge. I was happy for this to be the case as by the time it emerged I was 100% happy with who I was. I think the support I received, knowingly and unknowingly, from those around me helped me reach that stage of acceptance. Nobody made me feel like I wasn't normal and it was brilliant to be able to discuss my crushes as easily as they discussed theirs. I used to love Mondays so I could tell people about my weekend at the gay club, because it always seemed more interesting than what they were doing.

Of all my friends, the one I owe most to is the aforementioned best friend. He was there from the start and I think I was good for him too. We could sit and ogle at the television and magazines together. I just felt like one of the 'lads'.

As I have had such good reactions in the past, I don't know how I would react to receiving anything less. I can't imagine being in a situation where I would have to tell someone who would be anything but OK about it. All the friends I meet these days are either from the gay scene or like me and 'alternative'. Work is the only place where I would be cautious about revealing my sexuality but I hope when I get a full-time job I will be openly gay. I would hate to be spending 40 hours a week watching everything I say in case I slip up, and spinning endless lies.

As far as identity goes, I prefer to call myself a gay girl as opposed to a lesbian. Of course I am only going by the connotations of the word 'lesbian' e.g. the 'truck driver' look and the bulldog personality. I feel I am unsuited to being a lesbian. There is also a sense of sleaziness about the word. To me it suggests that lesbians sleep by day and only come out of their caves by night to entice anything female!

I look alternative and I don't associate that with my sexuality. It is more to do with the music I listen to. I have several piercings and a couple of tattoos which some would argue are 'lesbian' but not to me. I keep my hair long to stay away from the stereotypes of 'butch and femme'. I feel I do not fit accurately into either category so don't try to be one or the other. It's not that I'm scared to look like a lesbian for fear of being obvious to everyone, it just isn't my preferred look.

I don't have a specific type of girl that I'm interested in but I thought I might go for someone with piercings and tattoos too because a lot of people don't like how they look. My girlfriend has only four piercings. She only had one before I met her and we began talking because she liked my tattoos, etc. I used to go out with girls who disliked my piercings but I won't take them out for anyone. They are a huge part of who I am.

My girlfriend, Kerri [left of pic], is a lot more feminine than I am and that is great. We don't look like clones of each other and never will (luckily for her!). We are two completely different people and that's why we get on so well. We learn from each other. My girlfriend and I mean 'forever' to me. All my plans for the future include her and I know I am in hers also. While we are both our own people it is often good to be noticed as 'Kerri's girlfriend' or vice versa. I'm so in love with her that it feels so great to be associated with her.

Obviously marriage is off the agenda but we have talked about getting blessed and have said we will do it. We wanted to do it quite soon but expense has put us off and we want it to be perfect so we have a lot of saving to do! We don't feel we have to rush anything. We have our whole lives together.

So that's my story. I could tell you about all the great people I have met simply by being the sexuality that I am. I have the years of diaries to prove it! But as a final signing off I would just like to say: I love being gay. I love the life I lead because of it and I love the fantastic people I meet because of it.

Fiona Johnstone, 20, loves her home town of Aberdeen where she is studying publishing at university

The year was 1998

❋ Going away to university can be a turning point

I had just arrived in London as a university fresher. I was filled with excitement and anticipation. I had lived in Devon for most of my life and now I wanted to see what life was really like. University was the perfect opportunity to find a boyfriend and rid myself of the doubt that maybe men weren't quite my thing.

That night all the freshers gathered in the student union to meet each other and their 'parents' [other students who would help them settle in]. I failed to meet my 'dad' and ended up talking to a group of fresher blokes, one of whom I got on with very well. We talked for the rest of the evening about anything and everything. As a bloke he seemed perfect. Yet once again, as had happened several times in the past, I didn't feel attracted to him in the slightest. Just what was wrong?

For the past year or so I had felt like this about men. Every single one I met didn't do anything at all for me. I had even slept with a few, which was one of the biggest mistakes I ever made. That I might be a lesbian was just not an option. I had spent all my teenage years in Devon, where the only talk of homosexuality was homophobic. Two girls in my sixth form had once dared to kiss each other and had been seen. The result was threats of being beaten up. They were ignored and treated like dirt, treated as though they were infected with some horribly contagious and infectious disease. No, being gay was certainly not an option – convention at home said it was abnormal, so abnormal it was.

Freshers' fortnight continued in its own alcohol-fuelled and hedonistic way. Friends at home who wouldn't start university for another couple of weeks were eager for gossip. I was cross-questioned on the phone as to who I'd met, whether I'd met any nice blokes and if so, was anything going to happen. When I told them that yes, I had met a lovely bloke, but no nothing was going to happen, they wrote me off as mad and stupid etc. Conversations such as these ended with me trudging back to my room in deep thought as to what was happening.

I remember very well the day that everything became clear. It was a Sunday. I had gone out that morning, wandering about in half-thought, when the realisation hit me. Yes, I was gay. I couldn't hide from it any longer. The feeling was so strong and definite. I burst into tears, whether from relief or shock, I don't know. I made my way back, going over everything and realising how it all fell into place.

Someone once told me it was hardest to come out to yourself. I certainly thought so. I had spent so long denying everything, causing plenty of grief along the way. No matter how hard you try to convince yourself, the truth will finally come out.

I plucked up courage to phone my friends at home. I spoke to Laura first, knowing she would be the most difficult. I had no idea how to tell her, so after much rambling, I blurted out, "I'm gay."

Deadly pause. Then, incredulously, "You're what? You can't be!"

"Um, yeah, I'm pretty certain of it –" I was cut short.

"How could you do this to me? Why didn't you tell me earlier, instead of waiting until I'd just got to Uni to drop me right in it? I'm having a hard enough time as it is."

"I didn't know, did I? Anyway, I wouldn't have told you earlier because you were in a stress about Uni. I can't win, can I?"

"Charlotte, I'm sorry, but I'd rather wait until we go home to speak to you. I just can't deal with this at the moment."

"What! This is my problem, not yours! I am the same person as I was before, you know."

"I don't want to talk about it. I'll speak to you over Christmas. Bye."

I put the phone down, feeling furious, frustrated and miserable. She hadn't even tried to understand and there was no way I could explain things if she wouldn't speak to me. I had known her for six years. Surely she could have given me a bit of support or at least spoken to me.

After that scenario I waited until the next day to phone Becca. No idle chatter this time, I just told her straight out.

"It's fine," she answered, "doesn't worry me at all. As long as you're happy."

I breathed a sigh of relief and carried on chatting. OK, she may not have understood what was going on, but she was prepared to accept it. I had been terrified of rejection. Laura would have to be worked on. I didn't know how, but I wasn't giving up that easily.

In those early days I was extremely cautious of telling people at Uni. I didn't know anyone that well and didn't want to be given the cold shoulder by people before I even knew them. Life was difficult enough as it was.

The last night of freshers' fortnight was a ball. Something stuck in my mind about a deep and meaningful with Will (the bloke I met on the first night) about how we already felt we could tell each other anything. I decided to come out to him regardless of the consequences.

I went back to his place in South Woodford that night as I didn't want to go home on my own. I lay on Will's floor summoning up courage to tell him when out of the darkness I heard, "Charlie..."

"What?"

"I've got something to tell you."

"Go on."

"I'm bi..."

My face broke into a huge grin.

"Don't worry – I was just about to tell you something along those lines myself."

Huge hugs all round. He had been terrified of coming out to me so he told me he was bi, thinking I would be less likely to be frightened off. I wasn't the only one!

My two biggest fears were alleviated. Being rejected by everyone and feeling completely alone. Things could only improve.

But coming to terms with being gay isn't something that happens overnight. It took me another few months to be completely confident and comfortable with who I am. I didn't come out to many people as I still felt under-confident and anxious sometimes. I also had to get used to something else: getting into the scene. Walking into a crowded dyke bar when I didn't know anyone else was absolutely terrifying.

I returned full of confidence to London after a summer of having to live at home. Coming out was no longer a problem. Gossip travels fast at Uni and soon everyone knew about me. To this day I don't know who outed me. Even Laura came round after a few weeks. People see me as an individual first.

Coming out can be drawn out and traumatic. But you will get through it, even if you doubt yourself along the way or get hassled by people.

Now to solve my next problem – finding a girlfriend...

Charlotte Watson, 19, is studying medicine at St Bartholomew's Hospital, London. She wants to be a doctor and work with children

Keep it under wraps

There goes my girlfriend
Sat amongst her friends
No one knows a thing yet
Because that's what she wants.

Walking by myself
Trying to keep shtoom!
Not go over to her
To kiss her and say 'hi'

She wants to keep us quiet
Not tell a single soul
She wants me to tell no one
Yet meet her later on
We'll go up to my bedroom
And act just like a couple

Even though my parents know
Hers think we're just friends
Best mates says her mum
Oblivious to what's going on

Keep it under wraps she says

Her mum's a homophobe

Hannah, 16

Who's teaching who?

A student and her teacher talk with Jane Hoy about their lives and friendship

Sarah is nearly 18. Angela was her teacher at an education unit in London, for young people who are not going to school. They enjoyed working together at the unit, but it's only since Sarah left that they have felt able to become friends.

Jane: Sarah, tell me about yourself.

Sarah: That's a difficult question… I'm a student at college doing A-level biology; and I'm studying psychology and law at home with the National Extension College [a distance learning college]. It's cool working at home, I can organise myself better. I have bad sleeping habits which means I want to sleep during the day. I use the internet to keep in touch with friends I already know. I use it to find the latest news. I like it. It's more interactive and an alternative to TV. I socialise a lot more now. I go away a lot more. Go out drinking a lot more. I have more friends and we meet in each other's houses.

Jane: How would you describe your sexuality?

Sarah: Hmmm. Lots of younger girls say they are bi, but often they are just curious and turn out to be straight. You know, on the National Extension College course when I study psychology my tutor keeps telling me to write about my relationships with the opposite sex. It confuses me. I worry that I can't write what they want. I'll lose marks.

Angela: Yeah, they just assume you are straight.

Sarah: If I told the truth and wrote about my relationships with girls then I would have to come out to my tutor. I worry about coming out to people I don't know. If I came out in my college I'd be hurt. There's a biology technician who's gay – I've seen his boyfriend. I hear a lot of talk – in my class they joke about him. Really they are just curious but they make comments and sneer about 'poofs'.

Jane: Angela, how would you describe yourself?

Angela: As a teacher! [laughs] It's awful but I probably define myself by my work. I've been teaching for 18 years and worked at the Unit for nearly five. I enjoy teaching and helping students who are struggling to find their place in the world. Oh yes, I'm a musician and I enjoy singing and acting. I'm a student too – it's taken me 40 years to find out I can think, instead of panicking because I feel I am missing information. I value my friends and relationships. I have one friend I've known for 37 years. I'm studying for an MA in emotional factors in teaching and learning. I'm learning more about how unconscious things we do affect how we teach. I suppose this comes back to what Sarah was saying earlier about her psychology teacher.

Jane: How would you describe your sexuality?

Angela: I've veered – straight, lesbian, bisexual. I am on the 0-10 scale [from straight to lesbian]. When I've been in a relationship with a lesbian, very lesbian; with a man, very straight. [Laughs] But I still thought about women.

Sarah: I would be 10 on the scale!

Jane: When did you first think you might be lesbian?

Sarah: I met a lot of women on the internet and enjoyed their company. I told them I was a man because I didn't think I was a lesbian – I was confused. I wanted some friends. Some of the women fell in love with the person I said I was. It got sticky.

Jane: What happened?

Sarah: One of them flew over from America. It was awful. It [using the internet] went on for three years. I suppose some women were lonely. I got really hooked on the internet. Obsessed. I found it really hard to go out.

Jane: How did you work out you were a lesbian?

Sarah: I worked out I was a lesbian for other reasons. I was very attracted to women. I let myself be attracted.

Jane: When did you both meet?

Sarah: I came in, in my baseball hat.

Angela: Yes, Sarah came to look around the Unit.

Sarah: With my social worker.

Angela: We weren't sure Sarah should have a place, that she could manage getting up in the morning to get to the Unit. She was so depressed. But it was something Sarah wrote…

Sarah: God, I remember that. I wrote about my problems. I thought if I wrote about me, then you'd see what I was like and you wouldn't want me.

Angela: My first impression… there she was, head down, baseball hat… my gut feeling was Sarah might be a young lesbian. But I never assume.

Jane: Sarah, tell me about your interview for the Unit.

Sarah: It felt strange cos I'd never been interviewed. I think I did want to be there. I talked about my interests – I felt listened to.

Angela: You mentioned computers and American football. It was more like a chat – not the more formal thing. You talked about school and how your teachers made sarcastic comments about you not getting up in the morning. I was struck by how powerful one or two comments can be. They send you scuttling back and stop you in your tracks. Sarah was very anxious, suicidal and depressed.

Sarah: I made myself feel better by saying if everything went wrong I had a way out. I wasn't fitting in at school. I couldn't do what I wanted to do. I felt a mess. I woke up every morning feeling crap.

Jane: What made you feel like that?

Sarah: I suppose I was getting depressed because of school and being obsessed with the internet. I was having trouble growing up and being gay. I was angry. It was stressful for my mum. My family doesn't talk much about relationships. I got really fed up and needed to tell her [about being gay]. I tested it on my brother who was 13. I hinted and he started to pick it up. He was sweet. He offered to tell my mum for me! Mum's fine about it now. When I told her, it went on for three hours – we talked for ages. I said, "You know I have a lot of friends who are male but they are not close and I would feel weird if they were. I could never be with a man." She said, "Are you trying to tell me something?" I said I was gay. She gave me a hug. I felt weird because we don't usually talk. She came back home the other day and said, "Do you know that there is a whole book on lesbian and gay law?" I asked her not to tell my dad, but he took me out for a drink and started to tell me about gay women at his school. [He is a teacher.] He said it might be easier for them to come out in London. I said, "Oh, by the way, I'm a lesbian!" Then my friends found out!

Jane: How did that happen?

Sarah: It was at a party. I was followed round by a beautiful girl. She kept lying in front of me saying she was tired. We played truth or dare – I hadn't noticed a thing. I was embarrassed because she had been looking at me all night but I thought it was because she hated me. A really nice guy said to me in front of everyone, "Are you straight or lesbian?" They all giggled and screamed. Now I'm out, my friends tease me. Like my friend says, "Shall we have another Sarah outing party?" It's quite funny now. It's a weight off my mind. They are all great people. I saw her [girl on floor] a few times. Then I went back to my girlfriend and she went back to her boyfriend. But I hear she is with a girl now. I think she just wasn't ready.

Jane: How did the two of you get to be friends?

Angela: Sarah was the brightest and most challenging student I had ever met. I admit I was scared at first. I thought I might not be able to give her what she needs – I might not know enough. But then I realised what Sarah needed was a safe place and I could help. So I stopped worrying about me. At first Sarah dropped all sorts of hints but never said anything directly about what she wanted. She used to shout at me in our sessions. For Sarah, any attention, even bad attention, was important. She would hang round after lessons. Then she wouldn't come in in the morning, which was frustrating.

Sarah: Yeah well, when I was hurting myself I thought that if you really knew what I was like, you wouldn't like me.

Jane: **What were you hoping for?**
Sarah: To be me. Get angry. Be able to challenge people. Somewhere to be and explore things. I went in to the Unit cos I wanted to be around people.

Jane: **When did you first notice Angela?**
Sarah: Well, she was running around waving her hands!
[Angela and Sarah glance at each other and start to laugh]
Angela: Y'see, the Unit is an eccentric place. I think part of the appeal was that Alan [another teacher] and I used to make dreadful jokes. Sarah enjoyed the jokes.
Sarah: Yeah – it's important to have a laugh. Not talk about problems all the time. It was easier to wind Angela up and get to her. I seemed to be able to hit things and make her argue back. Things which were important to her.

Jane: **How did the two of you get to make a connection?**
Angela: We went on a field trip. Every hour Sarah used to tell me what expression was on my face. It was hard to relax. But I suppose Sarah was really telling me about her anxiety. We walked round and round a field and I asked her about her internet relationships. It made me realise someone needs a space to talk without labels and judgement. I suppose I was a bit scared round Sarah because I thought she saw through me. It made me feel vulnerable more than with other students – laid open. Sarah was accurate about my feelings – if I was angry, she would pick it up.

Jane: **How did you do that, Sarah?**
Sarah: My magical power! I liked to talk to Angela – can't remember why…
Angela: I listened, tried to just take in information she was giving me. Then I remember thinking something else was going on – a hint about Sarah's sexuality, just a possibility. I did think Sarah might need a positive role model, but I couldn't out myself – I suppose I wanted her to see it.

Jane: **So why couldn't you come out?**
Angela: Two things. I am not sure if it's appropriate for students to know about their teacher's sexuality. It's more important for students to experience themselves in relation to someone who is accepting of them rather than have to deal with your [the teacher's] sexuality. The important message is, don't judge. Talk about all forms of sexuality. I

think I would be prepared to go to court if I had to say straight marriage was the only acceptable form of relationship. We often had discussions about politics in the Unit. We had a boy who was a character and a half but he was constantly saying 'queer, battyboy' and so on. He brought in the Eminem CD – the uncut version which talks about raping lesbians. We had to make it clear his comments weren't appropriate, but use humour as well! His negative views brought issues of sexuality into the open. I don't think he really hated gays – he was just trying to get a reaction. But I often feel vulnerable because students are always asking me if I have a boyfriend.

Jane: Why does that make you feel vulnerable?
Angela: I think I am putting down my own sexuality. I try to fight against that. It would be honest to say I have a girlfriend or I am a lesbian. I can't do that because the prejudiced attitude towards gays and lesbians is that we are predatory and impose ourselves and our sexuality on young people. Heterosexuality is not seen in this way. Young people, especially gay ones, are assumed not to be capable of choosing for themselves.

Jane: Tell me more about why you couldn't tell Sarah about your sexuality.
Angela: I was really frightened by what the press said about that headmistress, Jane Brown. I was involved in supporting her campaign. She was the lesbian teacher who got really harassed in the press. She was supposed to have denied the children in her primary school the right to go to *Romeo and Juliet* because it was about a heterosexual relationship. Her experience really affected me. I was angry at the lies about her. The main reason she refused to support the trip was the cost of the tickets. Do you know she had death threats? It took ages for her to prove herself. I couldn't go through that. The other thing was that I remember being 16 and depressed. I suppose working with Sarah touched my own uncertainty about myself and I didn't want to unload this onto a young person.

Jane: When did you tell Sarah?
Angela: After Sarah left the Unit. It was more equal, Sarah was no longer a pupil – there wasn't the unequal power you have in school. We happened to be in the pub. Another teacher was there so I felt safe. You know, other teachers talked about their husbands – but I couldn't talk about myself because of the political situation. I have a really good male colleague who is straight but if kids try to wind him up and say he is a 'poof' he just says, yeah, he might be, so what? He tries to get them to think. This is helpful and supportive for me.
Sarah: I think Section 28 isn't right... Teachers don't step in when bullying is going on... But I think I would have been confused if teachers were out to me, though I wasn't in secondary school much.

Jane: What happened next?
Sarah: I was feeling better about myself. The first people I came out to, tested, were Angela and Alan [in the pub].
Angela: We were talking about secrets. I said I'd had relationships with men and women.
Sarah: We somehow got talking about relationships. Someone had had a baby. I said it would be difficult for me; I

was probably bisexual – boys didn't figure.

Jane: *What has made you keep in touch since then?*

Sarah: I was going to college but it was still nice to go back and see people I knew. People understood me. I go to stage school on Saturday now. I use the internet a bit. I like going with my friends to the Vespa Lounge [lesbian bar] and I like to talk.

Angela: Hey, you've forgotten the lizards.

[They both fall about laughing...]

Angela: That really cemented our friendship. Sarah has loads of real lizards, salamanders. I've only got a stuffed lizard on my keyring. She used to wash and mend it. She said he was being neglected.

Sarah: [rolls her eyes] Yeah!

Angela: Sarah came on our last school journey – she went as a support link between students and staff. When I get irritable with the students, she reminds me they're only 16. We were potholing, 'weaseling', going through cracks in rocks. My shoulder got jammed, I panicked and Sarah helped me through. She got me through it cos she had a flexible view and told me how to move.

Jane: *Will you stay in touch?*

Angela: I'd like to. I am anxious about Sarah's relationship. The first time you fall in love is hard. I need to know that Sarah is OK. She has a refreshing and creative view on life and I think talking to Sarah makes me realise how much I repress about myself.

Scared? Of course
I understand. Please sit.
What's the problem?
Oh really? Well that is
a problem.
Just brush it aside, it'll go away
Don't be silly, no one
actually feels like that.
Yes, I understand, but
that doesn't make it real.
Life is hard enough
without creating problems

Don't you agree?
Good.
It's a phase and we'll
get through it.
You know it's wrong
don't you?
Against your religion.
What would you family say? No, they wouldn't
understand
Gay indeed!

Stephanie Mann, 19, lives in Edinburgh and wrote
this poem just before she came out. She wants to be a writer

Suicidal

It was a revolution to turn to suicide. Now we are too apathetic. I don't mean to go on. I know what you are thinking. But hey, you are now on this sentence so you must be a little intrigued. It is difficult to maintain, you know – this angst-ridden post-pubescent behaviour. I'm nearly 21. Snap out of it. I can't. However I do have an excuse. We homosexuals tend to reach our sexual awareness puberty a little later in life so I will hang onto this angst a little later too. They go hand in hand.

All I see and hear are my own anxieties dancing like flames threatening to burn me the closer I get. I want to touch them, disperse them like smoke. They are not real. I don't need to live like this anymore but I am reassured by instability. Go with what you know, eh? Anyway back to the start. It was a revolution to turn to suicide. Oh the 90s. Now it is far too hackneyed. I don't need to be another kid you read about on some anonymous column, page 9 of the local paper. What'll I do? I'll probably end up writing about some anonymous kid in the column on page 9. What goes around comes around?

Nicola Wood, 21, lives in Glasgow, where she studies and writes

Listen to me!

What to do when your counsellor can't help

Lots of girls get very positive help and support from counsellors and therapists, others not so positive. Sam Lloyd is a lesbian counsellor working in a lesbian and gay voluntary project in Leicester. Her main clients are young lesbians or young women questioning their sexuality.

Here, Tina, Judy, Annette and Rachael (not their real names) talk to Sam about seeing a counsellor. Although they each had different backgrounds, they share the feeling of not being listened to and taken seriously – that their attempts to come to terms with their sexuality are explained away, or that the counsellor has an agenda of their own.

You might find yourself in a situation – with a counsellor, teacher, youth worker or social worker – which you think is not helpful, but perhaps you're not even sure why. Sam and our contributors have some ideas on how to make the situation work for you.

Tina is 23 and a lesbian. She has been in therapy since she was 17

I first went to see a counsellor at school. She didn't want to listen to my sexual thoughts about a female teacher. It was brushed aside and I felt that I couldn't talk about the huge emotional explosion that was going on inside of me. The feelings welled up so much, I cut myself to gain some release. Then I was sent to see someone else; I think he was a psychotherapist or something like that. He said that I needed a father figure. I thought he was just a dirty old man and refused to continue. Finally, I found this really good counsellor who was a lesbian. I fancied her a bit but she enabled me to talk about it and to think about why I had fallen for her. I even felt comfortable (ish) talking about sex.

Judy is 24 and first went to see a counsellor in her teens

The counsellor brought all my problems back to me being a lesbian. I got really fed up with that, it made me really mad. I felt that she could not really handle the fact that I was gay. I started to talk about how much I fancied this

older woman. Well, she really didn't seem to like this. It's funny, she started to ask me all these questions about my relationship with my father. You start to feel like they have got this hidden agenda. She also talked all of the time about the things that you do when you are young and experimenting. She never actually said, "It's just a phase you're going through," but you pick up things like that and I never felt that she took who I am seriously.

Annette

I remember talking to this counsellor and all of the time I was thinking, I bet she feels disgusted and shocked by what I am saying. I came out of there feeling really bad about myself. It was just something she put across, nothing she said, and she always smiled and looked friendly but really straight. I felt that she wanted to tell me that she was happily married.

Rachael

The counsellor I had was a lesbian and I thought, this is really great. She was what I call very out and proud. This was OK, I liked her and everything, but sometimes I just wanted to tell her that I hated the fact that I was a lesbian and I wanted to be 'normal'. But she just sat there with her pink triangle earrings and I thought, I can't tell her that I don't want to buy into being a right-on lesbian.

Sam Lloyd says:

If you have had similar experiences – perhaps you feel that your counsellor or therapist is not very comfortable with your sexuality or they are asking you about things that you don't feel are relevant – then ask them what they are getting at with some of their questions. If you feel you are not able to challenge them, you can always vote with your feet and don't go any more, or find someone else. See if there is a lesbian or gay counsellor or someone that other people recommend. Don't put up with a second-class service.

See Info zone for helplines, some of which can recommend counsellors

103

auntie fanny
& the agony gang

Q: Life's so hard, I'm depressed and I have these urges to harm myself

Jen: There's no easy way to get out of this – it might start with just hanging on and staying brave. This soon becomes other things. Soon you won't have to tell yourself to breathe in and out. It just comes naturally. I went through a period of depression. It took me nearly two years to get out of the pit I was in. It took all my guts and bravery to do it. I started to believe in myself.

Babs: I think everyone has the capacity to love themselves, not in a conceited way but in an energy-giving way that helps you be a significant person in the world and in other people's lives.

Gina: You are worth more. Think of your family and friends.

Charlene: Been there, done that. Stop. Think and reassess. You have too much to live for and UR loved by someone!

Tess: Get help. I have been in this situation and the only way out is to talk about it with someone who can help.

Kate: Life is too precious to throw away. It will always have its ups and downs.

Niki: Oh God, I've been there and done that and have come out the other side. Friends should offer support (not suggestions) and try to find a way of getting help without pressurising them into counselling or seeking medical attention unless the situation is getting dangerous.

Lee: No hot tips. Nothing ever worked for me except leaving school and going to college. I know that doesn't sound very positive.

Fran: Stay strong and always tell someone.

Getting grief at work

Amina and Andrea's stories are typical of what can happen to you at work if you are lesbian or bisexual. Both went through rough times at work. Both say that they couldn't have survived on their own. The trade union Unison and LAGER (Lesbian and Gay Employment Rights) helped them.

✳ Amina's story

Amina was 16, hoping to go to college, and working on Saturdays for a major shoe shop chain in London, selling shoes in their Oxford Street branch. One of the girls she worked with saw her kissing her girlfriend at Brixton tube after they came out of a nightclub. This girl told others and in the end the whole workforce knew. Some people didn't do or say anything and others started whispering rude comments into Amina's ears when management weren't watching. Amina became very distressed and contacted Lesbian and Gay Employment Rights (LAGER). They informed the management who arranged for Amina to be transferred to another branch and insisted that the staff in the Oxford Street branch all undergo anti-discrimination training.

✳ Andrea's story

Andrea worked at her local swimming pool as a lifeguard after school and on Saturdays. She liked her job and had many friends including those from the local young lesbian and gay group who would come and visit her at the pool. For over a month, a regular group of boys from the neighbourhood kept watching them and made no secret about the fact that they were prejudiced against lesbians. They used to follow Andrea round the pool till her friends had gone and then they would start making offensive gestures about her body and trying to wind her up. Andrea had joined Unison (Britain's biggest trade union) as soon as she got the job. She went to see her Unison shop steward who helped her write a letter of complaint and went with her to the meeting with her bosses where it was discussed. Because the local authority were committed to fighting discrimination they banned the boys from the pool for the rest of the year and thanked Andrea for raising the complaint which they realised took a lot of courage.

Case studies from Jocelyn Watson at LAGER. See also 'Work it out' in Info zone

Bus journey

I was just getting the last bus back from Leeds centre, where I'd been doing the gay bars. I went to sit down when I heard this voice: "Oi! Sara!" I turned round and it was one of my old school mates. He was sat with some lads. "I didn't recognise you in that shit, you look top." I smiled and went to join him. We talked about this and that. He kept commenting on how lovely I looked and asked if I had a boyfriend. I laughed and said, "I play tennis now." He and his friends didn't understand, they kept asking me what I meant. I just played with them and told them I don't play for the same team anymore.

The bus was packed and my stop was approaching. They were still not catching on. I stood up to get off, walked to the front of the bus. I turned round to a view of strangers and my friend and said, "In other words, I FUCK women!" I smiled and casually got off, trying not to look at the bus full of shocked people.

Sara, 19, lives in Leeds

tell all!

Someone told me that I was "the scum of the earth, nature's reject and damned to eternal life in hell". Well, I don't believe in God so the religious aspect didn't bother me. The bit about nature's reject is just rubbish because in nature over 50% of sentient species show signs of homosexuality. And as for the scum of the earth – well if they had come up with a more strongly argued and more eloquent argument, I might have been more upset. Why let them get to you when they are clearly not of an intellect to live and let live?

If someone calls me a fucking dyke or whatever, I just congratulate them on their powers of observation.

I was arm in arm with my girlfriend and we walked past some builders. One guy said, "Lez-be friends." We just burst out laughing because it was so pathetic.

A gay man said to me: "You don't look like a dyke! I said, "Neither do you!"

A guy shouted out: "I bet I could make you come with my dick better than a woman." I replied: "It's not the dick so much, I have no interest. It's the dick on the end of the dick."

Someone asked me what I do in the bedroom. I said, "The same as you only twice and better." How come people with closed minds open their mouths?

I was told that I was sick in the head; that I couldn't have kids because they would be screwed up, etc etc. I got very upset but argued my case. I would like to have stamped on their heads!

When men ask me what lesbians do in bed, I say, "Ask your wife."

When a man said to me that I was a lesbian because I just hadn't found the right man, I asked him what was so good about him that he'd be able to convert hundreds of thousands of gay women.

How do you deal with nasty comments?

girl 2 girl

Love, lust, loss

Photo by Itxaso Torrontegi-Palacios

* The first time I kissed a woman

The first time I kissed a woman I could have just collapsed. I had only been out for six months and had been in a long-term relationship with a guy, when I kissed a woman. There is no comparison. Your heart literally skips a beat. It felt like I had always imagined a kiss should feel. It was warm and tender, gentle. I'll never forget it. After that I couldn't wait to have sex with a woman and I can't begin to say the effect this had on me.

Stephanie Mann, 19, lives in Edinburgh

The lighting changes

The lighting changes, the mood is transformed.
I look at you. You're laughing with another.
You don't notice me. I'm just a no one.

I try so hard, but it's all lost.
Everyone thinks they feel the same as me.
They don't.
This is my love.

I'm not supposed to feel this way.
I've been told it's wrong.
Why is it wrong to feel like this?
I've tried to explain my feelings but they tell me it's not real.

I'm telling you, it's real.
When you talk to me, my other life seems futile.
What's the point of going on if you don't feel the way I do?
When you look at me, no one else is alive.

When you single me out, I know it won't be for long.
It feels like they all fade away.
It's just you and me.
I know you don't mean to, but you're ruling my life.

I do all that you want. I do more. I do more than I should.
No one understands me, the way I am.
I'm giving you my life, but you don't want it.
You don't know anything.

I watch you walking. I listen to you talking.
I need you to look at me,
But yet, when you do, I look away. I'm afraid.

I can't handle my love for you. It goes against what I'm meant to feel.
I need your love, maybe if you knew how I felt you might feel it too.
You're so special it hurts.

Nicola Sidgewick

This is my hand

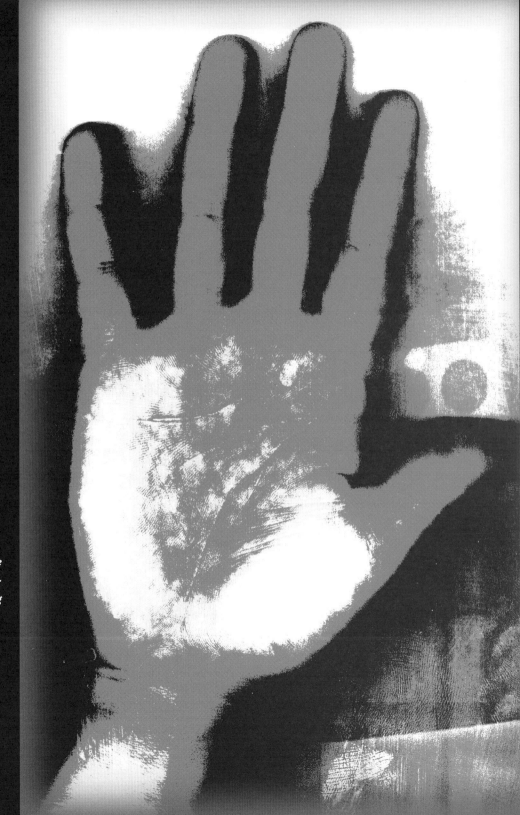

This is my hand
I dedicate it to you
These are my lines
And they are yours too
I have shadows also
And they are a shared joy

I take my eyes
And they follow you
I take my lips
And they speak for you
I take your hand
And we walk

Nicola Sidgewick is the Lesbian and Gay Society student representative at King Alfred's College, Winchester

WH Smiths bird

There's a girl who works in Smiths
She really is quite fit
It has to be said, I wouldn't say no
If she offered me a bit

That short blonde hair and sparkling eyes
Make my brain turn into mush
The slightest show of interest
And my girlfriend would get the push

All I need is a glimpse in the morning
It'll set me up for the day
If I had any say in the matter
I'd show her it's best to be gay!

Anna 'Stimpy' Stimpson is 21 and lives in Coventry where she works for Central Trains. She was raised with two older sisters in Staffordshire in what she calls a 'very homophobic' family. She writes poems, 'some serious and some less sensible,' with her best mate Debbie 'Tigger' Blakeman, who's 32

She

I feel her body is beautiful,
curved in all the right places.
For me she is the one,
a light in a thousand faces

I become immersed in her soul,
like I'm floating in the skies.
Her heart calls me back,
to the deepness of her eyes.

When we are together,
standing in the bright sun,
I could never feel alone,
because together we make one.

Stephanie Mann

Photo by Itxaso Torrontegi-Palacios

Class	Ticket type	Adult	Child
STD	CHEAPDY RTN CD	ONE	NIL	OUT

	Date	Number	
Y - P	27·AUG·99	17758	4779₴257M01

From	Valid	Price
NEWTON LE WILL *	AS ADVERTISED	£2·50M

To	Route	
MANCHESTER BR *		1015

Train Pulling

The first time I saw her was on a train
My stomach went all funny and so did my brain
She could only be described as one fit lass,
Now here she was waiting to check my pass.

I'd have given my number, but didn't dare
It's not a good move when your girlfriend's there.
I admit I had never seen her before
But I knew that I needed to see her some more.

So I rang up her station to try to attain
Where she was and to find out her name.
I left my number and waited to see
If she was as eager to contact me.

My phone went off shortly after midday
I felt so alive, so happy, so gay.
I know I shouldn't rush, but be patient and wait
But my plans may well change when I get my first date.

Anna Stimpson

116

*Three-way snog

It happened on a night out with the hockey team. We had just played the cup final and we went to a cheesy club in town. Spirits were high, even though we had lost. Something to do with the alcohol, I expect. The DJ was giving away bottles of champagne for random things like flashing your tits and then he said he would give one away to the first girls to snog in front of him. Before I could grab my nearest mate, a couple of Swedish birds had beaten us to it. He then said anyone who can top that gets the next bottle, so I got together with a couple of the hockey girls and we all snogged at the same time. Unfortunately the DJ didn't see or said he didn't so we had to do it again – oh what a shame! I was on a complete high for the rest of the evening because at the time I absolutely fancied the pants off both of the girls. You were asking what a three-way snog is like – well, noses get in the way a bit so it's mainly a tongue thing, lots of fun!

Babs grew up in Belfast. She is one of the few women studying engineering at Cambridge University, where she plays hockey for the second team (The Nomads), and hockey and rugby for her college. Sport helps her to stop thinking about work, relax, meet other girls and have a laugh

Forbidden love

My love is so deep
It hurts as I know
I cannot touch your lips
I am forbidden to look
into your eyes
and stare anything
which is not intended
as a gesture of the
passionate outburst of love
that I have for you.
This love keeps me from dreams
which do not allow me to
caress every part of you
which makes you the perfect
ray of light that I long to
connect with through both
body and mind

Amy Hanson, 16,
is studying for her A-levels in south London

8

As women we are sacred

As women we are sacred
No matter what our race
We like to nibble nipples
And have punani on our face
No matter how you like it
A finger or a fist
It's really quite terrific
And should never be missed
Emma with her whips and chains
Fran all sat in leather
But nothing can still quite describe
What we do with Heather
Really we don't give a shit
Cos we're so high on weed
And really, really freed.

Emma, Fran, Heather

Secret signs

Two bodies
As one
Moving together
In a singular motion
Rhyming with each other

The forbidden love that can't be closed
Is known
Sworn to enclosure they form as one

Meeting in difference
They are bound
To each other
Secret signs are passed
Crossing the barrier

They are joining together
In forbidden love

Nicola Wood lives in Glasgow. She is 21
and wrote this poem when she was 15

Charlotte

Child of night, my shivering soul you took
To hazy lands I'd never been before.
Ebony hair, your own enchanting look
Sublime beauty so rare I gasp for more.
But my love is not fearsome like a man,
Instead I am the quilt which comforts you.
I can't give you a gold ring like he can
Yet in your arms I know that this is true.
Never shall we hold hands in the cold street.
Never are we free from the shame and lies.
Never talk of you to the friends I meet.
Eternal gleam of sadness in your eyes.
And though the moon beams on us from her height,
Forever must we stay hidden by night.

Kate Holmes is studying English at Southampton University

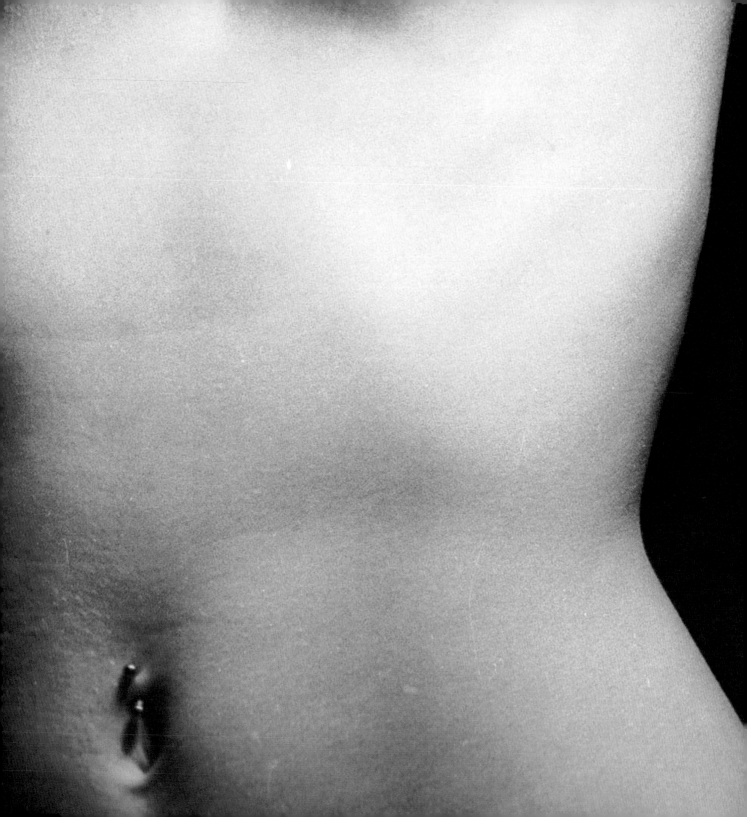

Now that 'us' is just me

Ageing years tore us apart
Unhappy, I sit here writing.

On cold winter evenings we'd exchange thick jumpers
On warm nights we'd help each other undress
Your cups of tea, white no sugar, my cups of coffee.
Under blankets of snow, we were still children.
Keeping you warm when we watched TV in my cold house.

Holding your hands to keep them warm when we shopped
Driving you home after a night together
Or falling asleep after a staying in.
Even the pizza place, they knew us.
We were an 'us', a happy us (most of the time)

It was like that until you shared someone else's jumper
In someone else's cold house.
You took her hand when you were cold
And it was her who made you tea.
Our blanket of snow turned to ice.
Our warmth became your warmth.

Sometimes I am reminded of you.
I hear a song that we once listened to together,
And I wonder how you are,
How your cups of tea taste, and if you smell the same.
If you're warm and yet strong enough to be you.
I wonder if you still listen to those songs, and watch those films.

But most of all, I wonder.
Do you think about me?

Joni wrote this when she was 16, she is now 18

**Photo by Itxaso Torrontegi-Palacios, a photography student at the University of Sunderland.
Itxaso is 21 and comes from Bilbao, Spain. She says photography can be a way to
see the world from new angles and let its contradictions co-exist.**

Bi-try in Belfast

When I was at home [in Belfast] over the holidays, I met up with some engineering friends. I had heard that a couple of the girls often snogged but thought nothing of it other than a wee bit of fun. I was talking to one of the girls and we ended up snogging in the nightclub. Actually we almost got chucked out by the bouncers cos someone complained – I guess that was my first experience of homophobia.

Anyway, I ended up spending the night with the girl and having lots of fun! The thing is, the girly had a boyfriend, so nothing was ever going to come of the relationship – or so I thought.

I met up with her another night and she introduced me to her boyfriend. One thing led to another and I ended up spending the night with both of them. I think large amounts of alcohol played a part in organising that one. We had a good laugh and in later conversations they told me that they would like it to happen more often.

I don't really know how to react to that one cos I have really strong feelings for the girl but just don't feel that way about her boyfriend. It begs the question, how much are you prepared to sacrifice for love? I haven't decided…

Babs

Superdyke

Julia Collar's story of how she grew to accept herself

In one careless afternoon I had left something more behind than a smear of blood on a sheet. Looking into his eyes I ought to have seen the heavens stretching away from me into sunset-washed happiness, but all I could think of was the aching, swelling delight that soon it would all be over and that the pain and fear would end. This should have been a moment incised into my life, cutting the child from the woman like Siamese twins joined at the head. I imagined that those first moments lying spent and gasping, looking at the child in me slipping away, would be difficult, but that I would recognise the potential my liberated flesh had to wield.

He held me so tightly afterwards. It was wonderful to lie like that because he was so huge and warm, he was my comfort and I loved him then because I did not have to look at him or talk to him, he was just there. It was almost like he knew and if he did, I am so grateful to him for putting his arms around me while the child and the woman both stopped breathing and died staring at each other coldly. I went down a hopeful adolescent and came out with nothing – there was nothing to be had and I had suspected it all along.

For a long time, though I wore make-up and an occasional skirt, I was not female. I'm not sure I was anything, I did not want to be male but I could not be female either. I was in some peculiar limbo where females are those who want men, who have breasts and shapely legs and soft hair, and know through and through that they are their gender and are at home in their bodies. I did not want men. I had breasts but they were scarred and hateful; I had shapely legs but it was muscle and grit that made them that way. I scraped all my soft hair away to raise money for charity; my school would have excluded me had I done it just for me – girls came with long hair, the male teachers liked it that way. So, I was a not-female, a nothing.

I came to accept being a nothing, the people who mattered most to me at that time loved me for it, I'm sure. I had a quick succession of female best friends with whom I was unbelievably close. Though these all ended painfully when they found boyfriends, I do not think I would have had a relationship with any of them had I not been a clothing, it was safer for us both because it meant we never reached the point where either of us realised that we were lovers.

Some of the ultra-feminine types at school, those with perms and nicotine stains on their fingers, bullied me chronically; I think they felt uncomfortable being around me but were not sure why. Fashion and trend meant conformity to their ideals and they led by example with new trainers, jackets, words and manners; it was a girl's world to which I did not belong and they hated me for it.

I covered myself in ammunition with baggy trousers and Doc Martens; I stomped around the corridors with so much attitude I'm surprised I could walk under the weight of it. The more they tore me down, the more I gave them to strip away, layering it on thicker and thicker over the cracks in my facade. It was such an effort to keep going back in every day yet somehow I managed it and eventually they got bored, or pregnant, and the gangs dwindled away.

University was a clean break. It was not meant to be, I expected that I would trundle along as before, playing consort to some whilst clearly marking the boundaries for others. I still did not know what I was but I was happier about it.

Most of the rooms in the corridor were occupied by the end of the first day and we were all planning to go down the student union to have a drink and get to know each other better. As we were about to leave we noticed that someone was moving into the end room: the door was propped open with crates of books and there were footsteps faltering up the stairs. She walked up the corridor behind her mum and dad, and, turning to face me, delivered a shy greeting.

Her hands were stuffed into her pockets but it felt like they were stuffed down my throat. I'm not sure even now what happened but in looking at her, an anxious and tired stranger, I knew her, knew everything about her, knew every inch of her body and mind, knew that there was a future here that would involve us both. It was not like déjà vu, I had not known her before, but it was more that her voice and presence channelled something straight into me that registered not only in my brain but in every cell, memory and sensation I had ever had or ever would have. She climbed inside me and looked me in the eye, my private and secret eye that saw but had not yet seen, she tickled a sensitive place deep within that I had covered with shame and terror because it threatened to make me feel like something. Here was beauty and power, playfulness and tenderness; I wanted to sink to the floor and cry because I was looking into a mirror whose reflection disturbed me with its inevitability.

She did not come down the bar that night; I was glad because I wanted to have time to mull over and relive the moment I met my match.

I remember another night that same week when we were sitting at the table in the shared kitchen just chatting and larking about. She kept on looking at me from under those splendidly long eyelashes and blushing as she giggled. She was so shy and reserved, giving nothing away – except that she was flirting with me. She was extraordinary, from her eccentric clothes to her slight but muscular figure – I could have died gazing at her bum while she flew around the cupboards and the cooker making pasta or cups of tea – to her mannerisms and quirks and the way she always looked dopey and sweet on her way back from the shower in the mornings.

When I went back to my room after we had all finally agreed to call it a night, I recall talking to myself about the fact that a lesbian fancied me. I asked myself how I felt about it. I replied that it was a bit scary but otherwise I was extremely happy. She was a lesbian. She wasn't wearing a rainbow ribbon and hadn't said as much but I could tell that she was reluctantly resigned to the fact that she was.

Guilt wafted between us as much as lust, we could probably have ended the painful yearning for one another just days later but we were not honest, it was too hard and I had not managed to grasp the reality of the situation: I knew I wanted her, but I did not know what it meant.

Months dragged by, months in which I became seriously depressed and began self-harming. I was a mess because I was so in love that it hurt me every time I looked at her and also because I would not let go of the mantra of hetero-sexuality that buzzed deep within me.

My dad is gay. My parents separated and then divorced because of it and Mum, though extremely tolerant of everything, was understandably homophobic when it came to her own family. You would have thought that having a gay parent might have made things easier but Dad and I were barely talking and Mum bore his sexuality with such shame that the taint stained through me as well. For years after we found out he was gay, we weren't allowed to dis cuss it, even in our home, and the few friends that I told were too tangled in the gleeful playground echoes of 'fag got!' and 'lezzie!' to believe what I said, let alone deal with it without showing revulsion.

I didn't want to disappoint or betray my Mum by admitting what (I came to realise) I had known since I was about seven or eight. It would appear to her as if I had lied all along, or else she would kick herself for being so blind.

We went for a weekend to Southampton, three of us from university in a youth hostel for a break before the exam season began. Standing on the deck of the *Victory* receiving the guided tour, I chanced to ask my love if she was enjoy ing herself. She reached for my arm and tugged me nearer to her, the smile on her face was like receiving the Holy Ghost and I felt something physically shift inside me. I knew that I had the ability to end this misery, there was a real possibility to be grasped, so I went home and wrote her a letter. It was the hardest thing I have ever done and the one she gave me in return must have matched my effort but we did it and tomorrow, 26 April, we celebrate two years of loving one another.

I had so many doubts in those first few weeks. That I loved her I was certain but at the back of my mind was the persistent thought that maybe it would be easier to stop this relationship and go back to standing on the margins. Holding another person in an honest and intimate commitment was a terrible and frightening prospect; there were real emotions involved that I had to participate in and no longer simply observe. She wanted my body to touch and to taste but it was so hard to give it to her, it still is because even now I'm struggling to work out who I am, how

Coming out is one thing but coming into yourself is another. My family has been so supportive despite my fears, in fact, a bouquet arrived from my mum just today to wish my love and me a happy anniversary. Many of my friends have been incredible too, it's surprising how much you can underestimate people, but I sometimes think that while our love is the best thing in my life, it has, by leaping straight into a serious and committed relationship, in some ways stopped me from going down the route of self-discovery.

I have never had a long-term relationship before and that is a learning curve in itself. While I think we have got each other and our lives all figured out, I still have not worked out exactly what I am. I know now that I enjoy being a woman, and I'm gradually learning to love my body with patience and the steady hand of my lover; sex is something I adore, it makes me feel real. Sometimes sex makes me cry because it is so beautiful and because I am so happy. I love to touch my partner and to make her gasp and stretch with pleasure, it can be a very powerful experience but mostly it is simply great fun! What I have with my lover I would not change for the world, she is everything that I want and need but there is someone else in our relationship too…

Lampeter is in the heart of west Wales and is Europe's smallest university and despite its size there is a wonderful melange of ethnicity, eccentricity and activity, rather like a microcosmic global village. There is also a thriving LGB [lesbian, gay and bisexual] community here. While it's great to know practically every queer in the place, there seems to be great pressure to stand up and be counted, to be out, to be an example of fearlessness and self-assurance in the midst of small town attitudes.

I am not very out. Family and friends is about as far as it goes. If I was walking down the street, I do not think anyone could tell and I suppose that's how it should be, why ram it down people's throats? Since coming out to myself however, I have wished that I had the courage to make the statement and talk about my partner openly without having to change the gender of my language, to walk down the street with her hand in mine, to kiss outside in daylight, to dance in the student union with her head on my shoulder and take advantage of the protection the union constitution affords us. All these things I want for us as a couple. What I want for me is to see people's reactions so I can learn to deal with it and deal with myself and maybe find out where I fit in somewhere along the way.

Establishing an identity is possibly the most important preoccupation of every dyke I've met, seen, or read whether consciously or unconsciously. Self-identity tends to be arrived at through mimicry and syncretism until a face is patched together that suits the personality and character of the individual. Everyone goes through this straight or queer, but if you're straight there are so many more references to choose from. Queer friends of mine, usually in a fond and dreamy reminiscence, tell of their early years of discovery when they hunted after poetry, novels, videos, television programmes, anything with queer content, comment and commitment, in the hope of learning about the possibilities and pitfalls of their being.

I'm still doing this now, as is my partner: she teases me about my obsession with kd lang and I tease her about Zoë Tate, but I think if we're honest, this searching is one of the most important activities within our lives at the

I went to my first LGB meeting in my second year. I went alone because my partner did not want to be out anywhere except in our home. I did not go back for quite some time. Here was a room full of people who were confident, knowledgeable and proud of who and what they were, a strength I could not match because there was no one I could identify with. When I finally did go back, it was because I was curious. There is one particular dyke on campus who fascinates both me and my partner. We ache to hear tales of her exploits and love to gossip with each other about what she wears or how she reacted to something. Barely knowing her is enough because we have built and embellished a whole imaginary character around her, complete with pedestal; we don't need her, we only need what she stands for.

It's not just that she's cute. It's that she's a specific variety of perfect. She's a miniature guru to us because she's so sure of her dykedom, so unshakeable and aggressive but still, beneath the scowl, there remains a chink of vulnerability like the knee that pokes alluringly through the rip in her jeans.

My partner and I have never been particularly bothered by the whole butch/femme thing but, in Lampeter, to be visible is very often to become a stereotype because that's what other people can most readily deal with and understand. She walks round in men's jeans with a bulge at the crotch, army boots, a baggy men's T-shirt and a wickedly short haircut. She loves women's politics, it's written in the dozens of earrings crammed into her lobes. She is fierce and makes comments about fucking women as often as she can manage whilst puffing wryly on a fag and suppressing a snarl. People are scared of her, most are nervous around her because she is bathed in sex, it sizzles round her like heatwaves, there is no doubt: she'll fuck you soon as look at you. She is magnificent. She is Butch. She is Superdyke.

It may have been the lure of an evening with Superdyke that enticed my partner to start coming to LGB meetings too. It didn't help that once we were there, Superdyke took an instant shine to my partner and proceeded to flirt with her all night. My skin crawled. I was so jealous. I was later informed by a friend that Superdyke had enquired whether my love was 'available' or not. I was worried: it must have looked like we weren't together.

If there's a lone dyke within five metres of my love then I start acting like I'm pissing on the four corners of my territory to keep the predator out; it's behaviour that I am ashamed of and that my partner hates. I am so paranoid, but then my love is extremely beautiful, extremely charming, and extremely unaware of the effect she has on other people; I'm terrified of losing her to a better dyke than me, a dyke who's out because she can be no other way and doesn't care what anyone thinks.

My love was not unreceptive to the Superdyke's flirtations, in fact every time I teased her about it she would blush and become angry because I had scratched a significant truth. Is Superdyke what my lover wants and is she only putting up with me? Or, is it that she is hoping one day I'll put on a rainbow-coloured crusader's cape just like Superdyke's and single-handedly save the world from homophobia by being so intimidating that people don't dare have an opinion, let alone voice it?

Eventually she admitted that she found Superdyke attractive, but trying to pinpoint how and why was much harder. My love described it as a kind of envy; Superdyke embodied everything that my love wanted to be herself, she wanted the swaggering confidence and certainty and the instant respect that blossomed wherever the Superdyke roamed. So Superdyke stands, hands on her hips, between us.

But if my love wanted an ounce of Superdyke then I wanted a ton. I am foolish, but if you could order Superdyke pyjamas with a great big 'S' emblazoned on the front and fake underpants in a toning colour sewn over the suit's trousers than I would run round the house in them to amuse myself and my partner every spare moment I have. I want to slip into her skin and let the river flow round me instead of through me, to move obstructions out of my path instead of weakly succumbing to them and dashing myself to pieces in my desperation.

This need wove itself into an intricate fantasy where I go to Superdyke's house. It is night. She lets me in without question because she thinks I have come to warn her to stay away from my lover. She sneaks me past her housemates who are watching television and into her room. Once there, I throw her down on the bed and without a word proceed to tear her clothes away and fuck her senseless before she has a chance to protest. She sees the rage in my eyes and reads it as hungry awe of her might, a votive offering at her temple. When she has come, slipping over my knuckles like a wedding ring, she turns to me to reciprocate my handiwork, but I rise from her like a burning sun through apocalyptic dawn and leave her lonely. I am carrying her starry crown with me as I proudly stalk the half-mile home. I burn to think of her lying confused and dazed on her pitiful bed as the realisation materialises that I have taken something away from her; she has lost her edge and is beaten at her own game.

It still makes me smile to think of it, I am not a cruel person but in Superdyke I lust to take her apart, break her down to prove to herself, if no one else, that she is just a woman underneath it all and can be bruised or pleasured the same as you or I.

Superdyke may seem the epitome of lesbian pride but she's all roar and no bite. Sometimes if you look into her eyes there's something really soft and feminine in there and, while I'm still angry with her for being everything I am not, I wish that I knew her well enough to hug her and whisper in her ear that pain and fear are part of life and that she is dealing with it as best she can. She looks for reassurance in other people's reactions but can she reassure herself?

The third figure in our bed is gradually warming up, it's the birth I've waited for and wanted. The child and the woman are now beginning to separate but it's the child's delight, creativity and bounce-back attitude that I want now and not the sophisticated mockery of a woman's high heels, wrinkles and stress levels! I find, however, that child and woman are not separating from each other, but from that big, warm, body that has lain behind me and held me tight on more than one occasion when I felt insecure.

All parts of me add up into that person I have not been able to face. Once it was a man, the first and only, he may have stroked away my virginity but he was also my confirmation that with his kind, no matter how gentle and caring, I could never find love and fulfilment. Most importantly he gave me a warm memory I have transformed into my growing confidence, something I am falling back into at last.

I don't need to turn round now because it is me who is the taller, broader, wiser body behind my partner and I hope that by holding her, reassuring her, that we can both gain the courage to go to gay bars, festivals, and even take magazines down from the shelves without thinking twice. I don't expect to feel this way about finding a place and identity forever. There's a life to be had above and beyond being a lesbian but right now it's like breathing again after choking, every breath is a relief.

Superdyke doesn't know it, but she's had a big impact on my self-perception. She's helped me grow into something more like me. I thought I was travelling onward, a linear journey into evolution, but really I'm coming back on myself. I've cut my hair short again now and it feels good to recognise my face again and to witness the teenager creeping back out even though I have left that age far behind. I think I was a lot more mature than I am now in some respects, my teenage years were the worst I've yet had but it was the events that ruined them – it wasn't my fault, I was OK. I have to admit that I was a Superdyke in my own right if I remember my dress sense and fuck-you attitude correctly, so really, in my Superdyke fantasies, I'm not so much taking the torch away from her but getting it back.

It's nearly midnight, almost our anniversary day. If it really is Superdyke who whets my love's appetite, and I really have gained my powers back, then I can't wait for her to see my pyjamas tonight!

Julia Collar is 21 and studying religious studies at Lampeter College, University of Wales

girl2girl

Info zone

In the Info zone you'll find answers to many of your questions. There's help if you're having trouble at work, followed by explanations of lots of queer words and then a directory of books to read, movies to watch, helplines to call and youth groups to join. But they're just a selection of what's on offer around the country and there's no substitute for finding out more for yourself...

Work it out

Getting hassle from workmates? Or just want to come out? You need some expert advice...

Thinking of coming out at work?

• Find out if there is an equal opportunities policy you can use to support you.

• Find out if you will you get support from other workers or from your supervisor.

• Call the lesbian employment rights helpline at LAGER (020 7704 8066). The experts there can give legal advice about work, including anti-lesbian or racist discrimination, contracts, health and safety, and pregnancy.

How can you tell if you are being discriminated against?

If you are being treated less favourably than other workers doing similar work, then you're being discriminated against.

What is sexual harassment?

• Unwelcome sexual comments or jokes

• Leering

• Unwanted insulting or rude comments

• Physical contact

• Unnecessary touching

• Any unwanted conduct of a sexual nature

You're being threatened with the sack. What can you do?

If you have been employed for more than one year in the same job, you may bring a claim for unfair dismissal if you believe you have been unfairly sacked.

Always:

• Get help. Don't go it alone.

• See if your colleagues or union can help.

• Don't take any action without legal advice.

• If you meet with your boss, take a union representative or reliable colleague.

• Keep a record – write everything down with dates, times, places, events, names.

• Collect all the evidence and file it safely.

• Tell your boss you want time to consider what has happened.

• Read your contract. If it's a verbal contract, ask for written terms.

• Check your employment rights.

• Try to get your boss to put things in writing.

Should I join a union?
Some unions have lesbian and gay networks and advisers

Lesbian and gay people are not protected from harassment by law, and the Trades Union Congress (TUC) is fighting to change this. Some unions have a lesbian and gay network – an example is Unison, which is a giant trade union for the public sector. Its lesbian and gay network helps people who want to come out safely at work, and holds meetings including national conferences. Black and disabled people in the network also have their own meetings. Some people are out at work, other people don't want to come out and don't want to be outed by anyone else.

Unions deal with a wide range of questions, including equal rights. Are the partners and families of lesbians and gay men given the same recognition as their straight colleagues? Do part-time workers have the same rights? Is the system of recruitment and promotion open and fair? Are cases of harassment being dealt with effectively?

Many young people, gay and straight, are poorly paid, and this issue has prompted Unison to run its 'Are you getting enough?' campaign. Don't forget, it's illegal for your boss to sack you for joining a union.

If you don't know which union to join, call the TUC on 020 7636 4030 and ask which is best for you

Student life
The National Union of Students campaign for 'legislative equality and wider social liberation' fights for the repeal of Section 28 and the lowering of the age of consent for gay men. The NUS represents individual lesbian, gay and bisexual students and helps student branches to set up new LGB groups.

You can get information on your local college lesbian, gay and bisexual groups or the lesbian, gay and bisexual campaign from NUS, 461 Holloway Rd, London N7 6LJ. 020 7272 8900. Email nusuk@nus.org.uk   website www.nus.org.uk

Words

The meanings of words change over time, so check out with people what they want to call themselves. Some words that have been insults get reclaimed to be used with pride – some lesbians call themselves dykes, for instance – but that doesn't make it OK for straight people to use those words.

Age of consent
The age when the law says you're responsible enough to have sex. In the UK the age for straight sex is 16 and this includes lesbian sex by default. The age for gay men is, unfairly, 18.

AIDS (Acquired Immune Deficiency Syndrome)
AIDS is not a disease, it's a syndrome or set of symptoms following damage to the body's immune system, caused by the HIV virus.

Batty boy, shirtlifter, faggot, sissy, cocksucker
Insulting words for gay men.

Bicycle, swings both ways
Insulting words for bisexual people.

Bisexual
A man or woman who fancies people of either sex.

Black triangle
A symbol of anti-social behaviour, some lesbians were forced to wear this badge in Nazi concentration camps in the second world war and it is now seen as a sign of lesbian strength alongside the pink triangle for gay men.

Butch
Some lesbians who feel masculine or enjoy their boyish side call themselves butch.

Closet
Someone who's 'in the closet' is lesbian, gay or bi, but not open about it.

Coming out
The term used by lesbians, gay men and bisexuals to describe their experience of discovery and acceptance of their sexual orientation and their decision to share this with others when and how they choose.

Drag king
A woman who dresses up in male clothes for a special occasion for theatrical effect.

Dyke
Reclaimed by lesbians but originally an insult.

Femme

Some lesbians who enjoy or play up their femininity call themselves femme.

Gay

Is a man or woman who is sexually and emotionally attracted to people of the same sex. Some gay men prefer to be called 'gay' rather than homosexual; some women prefer 'lesbian'.

Heterosexism

Prejudice in favour of heterosexual relationships and against lesbian, gay and bisexual ones.

Heterosexual

A person who's only attracted to the opposite sex.

HIV (Human Immunodeficiency Virus)

HIV is a fragile virus which attacks the body's immune system (its defence against disease) and can lead to AIDS. The virus exists in many body fluids but only in blood, semen and vaginal fluid in enough quantities to be able to infect another person if it gets into their bloodstream. It can only be passed on through anal or vaginal intercourse with a man who doesn't use a condom, transfusions of infected blood, reuse of needles and syringes (drug use) and from mother to baby. Many people living with HIV remain healthy and do not develop AIDS-related illnesses.

Homophobia

Fear and hatred of lesbian, gay and bi people.

Homosexual

Someone who fancies people of the same sex.

Internalised homophobia

Hating your own lesbianism or bisexuality because you've picked up so much negative stuff about lesbians (from prejudiced people) that you don't want to be one.

Kush

A Hindi and Urdu word for gay used in India, and now in Britain, by South Asian lesbians and gay men.

Labrys

Double-headed axe worn as an earring or on a necklace, ancient Greek symbol of strength, sometimes worn by lesbians.

Lemon, les be friends, lezzie

Insulting words for lesbians.

Lesbian

A woman who only or mainly fancies women. The word comes from the Greek island of Lesbos where a poet called Sappho ran a school for girls and wrote love poems to women, in ancient times.

Poof, poofter and queen

Insulting words for gay men, which some gay men reclaim to use about themselves.

Queer

A term mainly for gay men which was an insult but is being reclaimed – some lesbians use it about themselves too and it is sometimes used to include all those lesbian, gay, bi and trans people who are happy to be different.

Rainbow flag/ freedom flag

A flag in rainbow stripes which symbolises the spectrum of sexuality and therefore lesbian and gay pride. Rainbow flags and stickers outside a pub or shop mean it welcomes gay people.

Safe sex

This means keeping yourself healthy if you are having sex/making love. Women having sex with women have less chance of picking up sexually transmitted diseases (STDs), or vaginal infections like thrush. If you have sex with a man, you should use condoms or femidoms and a water-based lubricant like KY jelly to reduce the risk of disease or pregnancy. There is a high risk of catching HIV if you have unprotected vaginal or anal intercourse with a man (fucking without a condom), or share works (needles and syringes for drugs) with a man or woman, if one of them has HIV. There's a low risk of transferring the virus between women during sex. There's a low risk from masturbating each other or from oral sex with a man or a woman. To make sure you can both stay happy and safe, it's a good idea to talk about sex openly. Don't do anything you don't want to do. Wash your hands and if you use sex toys (vibrators, dildos) wash them too, before sex and before swapping around. Touching, kissing, holding, hugging and fingering are all safe, fun and loving things to do. More info from the health organisations in the listings, later in this section.

Section 28

Clause of the 1988 Local Government Bill which tried to prevent local authorities from using public funds to 'promote' homosexuality, either directly or through financing other groups. So far no prosecutions have been brought but some local authorities have refused to fund lesbian and gay projects. The threat of prosecution has been enough to stop some schools and youth projects openly supporting young lesbian, gay and bisexual people. Repealed in Scotland in but not elsewhere in the UK as at August 2000.

Straight

A slangy word for heterosexuals.

Transsexual/transgender

Someone who has a girl's body but feels like a boy, or vice versa. If they choose, they can have medical treatment and surgery to change their body. First they have counselling to see if it's the right thing for that person.

Zami

A word from the Caribbean used by writer Audre Lorde to describe black lesbians who have one or both parents from Africa, Caribbean or Asia.

Look in!

Shopping

DIVA MAIL ORDER Books and videos. 3 Broadbent Close, London N6 5GG. 020 8340 8644.

GAY'S THE WORD BOOKSHOP 66 Marchmont St, London WC1N 1AB. 020 7278 7654.

LIBERTAS! Women's Bookshop and cafe. 42 Gillygate, York YO31 7EQ. 01904 625522. Mail-order service: books@libertas.co.uk or www.libertas.co.uk

SILVERMOON WOMEN'S BOOKSHOP 64-68 Charing Cross Road, London WC2H 0BT. 020 7836 7906.

IN OTHER WORDS lesbian run bookshop 64 Mutley Plain, Plymouth, Devon PL4 6LF. 01752 663889

OUT! lesbian and gay bookshop. 4/7 Dorset St, off Edward St, Brighton BN2 1WA. 01273 623356.

Books and films

*Some of these books and films have been recommended by contributors,
others by bookshops who told us what their customers enjoyed*

✳ Fiction

Alison Bechdel, *Dykes to Watch Out For* (Firebrand). First in a series of cartoon books about a bunch of lesbian pals in the USA. Funny, astute and addictive – especially the latest books in the series.

Rita Mae Brown, *Rubyfruit Jungle* (Penguin). Set in the 1960s in the southern states of the USA, Molly is adopted by a poor couple. As she grows up she realises she is different – and won't apologise.

Paula Boock, *Dare, Truth or Promise* (Women's Press). Dramatic love story about questioning your sexuality and the pain of separation.

Sarah Dreher, *Stoner McTavish* (Women's Press). First in a series of crime thrillers in which the heroine, a lesbian travel agent, gets involved in all sort of affairs, mysterious and otherwise.

Stella Duffy, *Beneath the Blonde* (Serpent's Tail). One of a series of crime thrillers featuring Saz, South London's most feisty private eye. She's got the job of protecting gorgeous lead singer Siobhan, threatened by a stalker.

Emma Donoghue, *Stir-fry* (Penguin). The story of how a young student in Dublin, Maria, comes to terms with her own sexuality when she goes flat-hunting and finds herself sharing with two women who are lesbians.

Val McDermid, *Report for Murder* (Women's Press). One of a series of crime thrillers. Lindsay Gordon, lefty, lesbian tabloid journalist, investigates the murder of a public school pupil at a gala fundraising concert.

Lindsey Elder (editor), *Early Embraces* (Alyson). True life stories from the US of women describing their first lesbian experience, the joys, fears, confusions and emotions of starting up a relationship.

Nancy Garden, *Annie on my Mind* (Aerial). Powerful emotional story of two girls who fall in love at school and how they confront the hatred and fear of students and teachers.

Patricia Highsmith, *Carol* (Bloomsbury). A young shop assistant falls for an older woman.

Isabel Miller, *Patience and Sarah* (Women's Press). Historical love story set in 19th century Connecticut.

Alice Walker, *The Color Purple* (Women's Press). Extraordinary tale of a young black American woman's struggle against rape, fear and a brutal marriage. She has no one to talk to but God until she meets a woman who offers love and support.

Oscar Wilde, *Complete Works*. Stories, poems and plays by the famous Irish playwright who was sent to jail in England for a gay affair in the 19th century.

Sarah Schulman, any of her novels which are set among New York's dropouts and queer folk.

Sarah Waters, *Tipping the Velvet* (Virago). Saucy and exciting historical novel set at the end of the 19th century. The story of 18-year-old oyster girl Nancy and her adventures after she leaves her home in Whitstable, Kent, falls in love with a music-hall male impersonator and hits the highs and lows of life in Suffragette London.

Jeanette Winterson, *Oranges Are Not the Only Fruit* (Vintage). Vivid story set in the north of England of a young woman coming to terms with her sexuality and struggling with her fundamentalist Christian mother and her friends; also on video.

✳ *Poetry*

Carol Ann Duffy, *Meantime* (Anvil Press). Includes poems about love and everyday life.

Jackie Kay, *The Adoption Papers* (Bloodaxe). Gives voice to all the different characters involved when a black girl is adopted by a white woman in Scotland.

✳ *Lives*

Chastity Bono, *Family Outing* (Pan). A memoir of Chastity's coming out as a lesbian to her famous parents (Sonny and Cher), their relationship and a look at the difficulties she faced when she came out. Also contains interviews with other parents of lesbian and gay children in the USA.

Rose Collis, *Portraits to the Wall* (Cassell). Fascinating and easy to read histories of famous lesbian characters in Britain and Europe including stars like Greta Garbo

Ellen Degeneres, *My Point and I Do Have One* (Bantam). Comedian Ellen wrote this before she came out.

Betty Degeneres, *Love, Ellen* (Rob Weisbach Books) Ellen's mother describes her reactions to her daughter's sexuality and explores the growth of her acceptance and friendship with her daughter.

Barbara Bell, *Just Take Your Frock Off* (Ourstory) Hilarious, engrossing and often sad story of Barbara, born in the north of England around 1914. She charts her life as a lively loving lesbian through lots of relationships, the police force, teaching, buddying people with AIDS and retirement in Brighton in the 80s.

Mary L Gray, *In Your Face: Stories of the lives of queer lesbian, gay and bisexual youth* (Harrington Park Press). Collection of interviews with young people in the USA on their views about gender and sexuality.

Emma Healey, *Lesbian Sex Wars* (Virago). A readable introduction to arguments over sexual freedom in the lesbian community over the last twenty years in Britain.

Audre Lorde, *Zami: A new spelling of my name* (Pandora). Classic autobiography. Follows a young black girl growing up in 1930s Harlem and the women around her.

Valerie Mason-John (editor), *Talking Black* (Cassell). Anthology of writings by lesbians of black or Asian descent living in Britain. Topics include coming out, domestic violence, relationships with white women and the contributions of black lesbians to the gay community.

Zachary Nataf, *Lesbians Talk Transgender* (Scarlet Press). Short and readable account from the female-to-male transgendered author based on extracts from interviews with lesbians about bisexuality and transgender.

Lindsey Van Gelder & Pamela Robin Brandt, *The Girls Next Door: Into the heart of lesbian America* (Touchstone). Witty, fun yet thought-provoking account from two women who took a trip across America and interviewed a lot of lesbians living very different lives on the way.

✳ *Information*

David B Taylor, *Homosexuality, the Bible and the Fundamentalist Tradition*. A critical view of how the Bible is often misused. Mail order from the Lesbian and Gay Christian Movement address in the National Organisations list below.

Parents' Friend, *Guide for parents who have lesbian, gay or bisexual children*. A booklet with answers to all the questions you ever wanted to ask. Available mail order from the Parent's Friend address in the National Organisations list below.

Newspapers & Magazines

Boadicea Newsletter for lesbians with disabilities c/o GLAD 336 Brixton Rd, London SW9 7AA. 020 7346 5800

Diva National monthly lesbian magazine from newsagents or by subscription: 020 8348 9967 (international +44 20 8348 9967)

GCN Gay Community News; reflecting Irish lesbian and gay life today. Free monthly newspaper. Website www.gcn.ie email gcn@eircom.net

GScene For the Brighton area. Email gscene@mistral.co.uk

Outback Newsletter Listings, information, contacts for Cornwall. PO Box 41, Penzance, Cornwall TR18 2XY

Pink Paper Free national UK weekly newspaper from lesbian and gay venues and some libraries

ScotsGay For lesbians and gay men in Scotland. Website www.scotsgay.co.uk

Shout! Free weekly newspaper in Leeds

Zone For Shrewsbury and the surrounding area

Film & video

2 Seconds (15) For romantics, winners, losers, cyclists or anyone who likes fast-paced comedies and twists of fate.

All Over Me (15) Claude and Ellen are best friends who live in a not-so-nice area of New York. They are involved in the subculture of 1990s youth but all is changed one night when a violent and meaningless death rocks their lives.

Better than Chocolate (15) Joyful US lesbian romantic comedy.

Beautiful Thing (15) Coming out story about two teenage boys on a Thamesmead council estate. Funny and tender.

Fire (15) Set in India where two sisters-in-law, neglected by their husbands, fall in love.

The Incredibly True Adventures of Two Girls in Love (15) Teenage comedy. Randy, a working-class tomboy, meets the beautiful well-to-do Evie, and the two girls (one white, the other mixed-race) discover first love.

Love and Other Catastrophes (15) Enjoyable Australian campus movie, where lesbians are just part of everyday life.

Ma Vie En Rose (My Life In Pink) (12) Witty and moving story about a small boy who likes to dress in girls' clothes.

My Beautiful Laundrette (15) White skinhead gets off with Asian gay boy to the disgust of their families and friends.

Oranges Are Not the Only Fruit (15) The television version of Jeanette Winterson's novel (see above).

Salmonberries (15) kd lang as you've never seen her before plays a young lesbian in sad love story.

Show Me Love (15) Elin and Agnes both yearn for more than their school and the small town of Amal, in Sweden, can ever seem to offer. But they find out how much they have in common on the night of Agnes's party.

Why Not Me? (Pourquoi Pas Moi?) (15) Young French lesbians and their gay male friend all decide to come out to their parents at the same time. There are some surprises in store.

Stonewall (15) Powerful and moving documentary of the struggle for lesbian, gay and trans people's rights in the US.

For older viewers

Bar Girls (18) A fresh romantic comedy. Lives and loves intertwine against the backdrop of a Los Angeles lesbian bar.

Bound (18) Raunchy gangster movie in which the main characters are a lesbian and a bi woman who get together.

Boys Don't Cry (18) True story of a girl who lived as a boy in smalltown America but paid a terrible price.

Chasing Amy (18) Alternative US romantic comedy has straight guy falling for queer gal.

Chutney Popcorn Comedy about an Asian family in the USA who all try to get on with each other despite their differences, including lesbians and gays in the family.

Desert Hearts (18) Sad love story set in the American south where an older woman meets a moody young lesbian.

Go Fish (18) Fun with a crowd of American dykes.

High Art (18) Artists and their angst. Slow, moody and tragic.

Set It Off (18) Exciting but tragic action movie about a gang of poor black American women (including rap star Queen Latifah as a lesbian) who become bank robbers to support their families.

Watermelon Woman A black American dyke goes looking for her predecessors in the film industry while sparring with friends and lovers. Funny and thought-provoking.

Top row: Stills taken from the film *All Over Me* courtesy of Millivres Multimedia
Bottom row: Taken from the film Set It Off, an Entertainment Release by D. Stevens

National organisations

ALBERT KENNEDY TRUST Help with housing for homeless lesbian and gay young people. Unit 305A, 16/16a Baldwin Gdns, EC1N 7RJ. 020 7831 6562. Manchester Office: 0161 228 3308, lesbians 0161 228 1294

ANDROGYNE For 'third gender' information, send an SAE to BM Androgyne, London WC1N 3XX

BROTHERS AND SISTERS For deaf lesbians and gay men. Minicom 020 7837 5561

DFLAG Federation of Deaf L&G Groups, 71 Victoria Ave, South Croydon, Surrey CR2 0QP

FTM NETWORK For female-to-male transsexuals. BM Network, London, WC1N 3XX. Helpline 0161 432 1915, Weds 8pm-10.30pm

CHILDLINE 0800 1111

GEMMA Lesbian and bi women with/without disabilities. BM Box 5700, WC1N 3XX

LAGER Lesbian & Gay Employment Rights, Leroy House (Unit 1G), 436 Essex Road, London N1 3QP. Lesbian helpline 020 7704 8066, fax 020 7704 6067. Website www.lager.dircon.co.uk

LESBIAN AND GAY CHRISTIAN MOVEMENT (LGCM) Includes women's network. Oxford House, Derbyshire St, London E2 6HG. 0207 739 1249. Counselling helpline 020 7739 8134. Website members@aol.com/lgcm email lgcm@aol.com

LONDON LESBIAN AND GAY SWITCHBOARD Phone from anywhere in the country to get help, advice or details of local groups. PO Box 7324, London N1 9QS. 020 7837 7324 (24hrs)

LYSIS Young Lesbian Information Service, PO Box 8, Todmorden, Lancashire OL14 5TZ

MERMAIDS Transgender information for children and young people, BM Mermaids, London WC1N 3XX. Website www.mermaids.freeuk.com

NATIONAL FREEDOM YOUTH For LGBT under 26. Send an SAE to PO Box 72, London HA5 2UJ

NATIONAL FRIEND Information about local lesbian lines, switchboards and Friend groups in the British Isles. 0121 684 1261

NATIONAL UNION OF STUDENTS (NUS) Information on your local college lesbian, gay and bisexual networks or the national campaign from NUS, 461 Holloway Rd, London N7 6LJ. 020 7272 8900. Email nusuk@nus.org.uk website www.nus.org.uk

NATIONAL YOUTH AGENCY Resources for teachers and youth workers. Information Team, National Youth Agency, 17-23 Albion St, Leicester LE1 6GD. 0116 285 3700. Email carolyno@nya.org.uk

PARENTS' FRIEND For families and carers of gay and lesbian young people. WVSC 2/3 Bell St, Wolverhampton WV1 2PR. Helpline 01902 820 497. Website www.parentsfriend.demon.co.uk

POSITIVELY WOMEN Support for women with HIV or AIDS. 347 City Rd, London EC1V 1LR. Mon-Fri 10am-4pm

020 7713 0222

PRESS FOR CHANGE Campaigning group for transgender people and their rights. BM Network, London, WC1N 3XX. Website www.pfc.org.uk

QUAKER LESBIAN AND GAY FELLOWSHIP 3 Hallsfield, Swindon SN6 6LR

RAINBOW NETWORK lesbian, gay and bi website for the UK www.rainbownetwork.com

RAPE CRISIS CENTRE Call directory enquiries on 192 for your local centre/helpline

REGARD For lesbians & gay men with disabilities. Unit 2J, Leroy House, 436 Essex Road, London N1 3QP. 020 7688 4111, fax 020 7688 4114. Website www.regard.dircon.co.uk email regard@dircon.co.uk

SAMARITANS 08457 909090

SCHOOL'S OUT! Lesbian and gay teachers and school students. BM School's Out, National, London WC1N 3XX. Email: secretary@schools-out.org.uk website: www.schools-out.org.uk

SHAKTI Lesbians and gay men of Asian descent. BM Box 3167, London WC1N 3XX

STONEWALL Campaigns for lesbian and gay rights, including the repeal of Section 28, changes to immigration laws and the age of consent for gay men. 16-17 Clerkenwell Close, London EC1R 0DY. 020 7336 8860

STONEWALL HOUSING ADVICE For young lesbians and gays. 020 7359 5767

TERRENCE HIGGINS TRUST For advice and information on HIV. 52-54 Grays Inn Rd, London WC1X 8JU. Helpline 020 7242 1010

TRADES UNION CONGRESS Information on which union to join. 020 7636 4030

VIGOUR Support group for visually impaired gay men and women. Free taped newsletter/magazine service including excerpts from *Diva* magazine. Email: vigouruk@hotmail.com

WOMEN'S HEALTH For all health enquiries. 52 Featherstone St, London EC1Y 8RT. Helpline Mon-Fri 9.30am-1.30pm 020 7251 6580

YOUTH ASSISTANCE ORGANIZATION American website for lots of stuff of interest to LGB young people. www.youth.org

London general

AMACH LINN Irish lesbians & gay men in London. c/o Hammersmith Irish Centre, Blacks Rd, Hammersmith, London W6 9DT. Helpline Tue/Wed 7.30-9.30pm 020 8569 7500

AUDRE LORDE CLINIC Lesbian sexual health clinic. The Royal London Hospital, Ambrose King Centre, Whitechapel Road, London E1 1BB. Clinic Friday 10-5pm. 020 7377 7312

BISEXUAL HELPLINE Tues-Wed 7.30-9.30pm, Sat 10.30-12.30pm 020 8569 7500

BLACK LESBIAN & GAY CENTRE For people of African, Caribbean and Asian descent Room 113, 5/5a Westminster Bridge Rd, London SE1. 020 7620 3885

DIASPORA For black and minority ethnic lesbian, gay and bisexual young people. 020 8533 2174

GALOP For lesbians, gay men and bisexuals facing homophobic violence or dealing with the police. 2G Leroy House, 436 Essex Road, London N1 3QP. Helpline 020 7704 2040

JEWISH LESBIAN AND GAY HELPLINE Mon and Thurs 020 7706 3123

KISS The Naz Project for lesbian and bisexual young women from the Asian community. 241 King St, London W6 9LP. 020 8741 1879

LESBIANLINE Advice, information & support. Mon & Fri 2-10pm, Tu-Thurs 7-10pm 020 7251 6911, Minicom 020 7253 0924

LLGBT London Lesbian, Gay & Bisexual Teenage Group, 6-9 Manor Gardens, Holloway, London N7.Wednesday 7-10pm Sunday 4-7pm 020 7263 5932. Website www.teenagegroup.home.ml.org

LONDON CONNECTION For homeless and/or unemployed lesbians and gay men aged 16-25. Thursdays 6-9pm. 12 Adelaide Street, London WC2N 4HW. 020 7766 5550

LONDON FRIEND Social and support centre for anyone coming out. 86 Caledonian Rd, London N1 9DN. 7.30-10pm 020 7837 3337

LONDON LESBIAN AND GAY SWITCHBOARD Helpline for advice, support or just a chat. 020 7837 7324 (24hrs)

LONDON YOUTH Umbrella organisation for London youth work Bridge House Bridge House Key Preston Road London E14 9QA. 020 8537 2777

MUSLIM GROUP Friendly and supportive new lesbian and gay group with active women members. Al Fatiha – London, Number 424, 37 Store St, London WC1. Email alfatiha_london@hotmail.com

PACE Counselling for lesbian, bisexual and gay individuals and groups. 34 Hartham Rd, London N7 6DL. 020 7700 1323

London youth groups

CAMDEN Diverse Divas for 25 and under, lesbian & bi women meet Mon 6-9pm. 020 7267 8595

HOUNSLOW Horizons project for young lesbian and bisexual women under 25. Sunday 6-8pm 07956 459 223

Islington North London Line for young lesbian and bisexual under 25s. Block H Barnsbury Complex, Offord Rd, London N1 1QG. 11-6pm 020 7607 8346

GREENWICH Freedom Youth Woolwich Common Project. 248-266 Nightingale Vale, Woolwich Common Estate, London SE8 4HN. 020 8316 4397

Metro Youth for young lesbians, bisexuals and gay men including a group for the under-16s. Unit 401, 49 Greenwich High Road, London SE10 8JL. 020 8265 3311, helpline 7-10pm 020 8265 3355. Website: www.themetro.dircon.co.uk

HACKNEY Staying Out Project for lesbians, gay men and bisexuals under 26. Meetings for under 16s. Vernon Hall, Florfield Road, London E8 1DT. 020 8533 2174

HARINGEY Girl Diva for lesbian and bisexual under-25s, and One Up mixed group for under-18s. 020 8348 1785

HARROW QT youth group for gay, lesbian and bisexual young people aged 16-25 in the Watford and Harrow area. Fri 6-10pm 020 8427 1799

HILLINGDON SNAP Youth Group for lesbians, gay men and bisexuals under 23. Weekdays 9am-6pm 020 8289 6698

Lesbian, Gay and Bisexual Youth Group Youth and Community Service, Civic Centre 3S/07, Uxbridge UB8 1UW. Sun 6.30-9.30pm 07801 967692

KENSINGTON & CHELSEA Notting Hill lesbian and gay youth project for under-25s. 5b Denbigh Road, London W11. 020 7229 3266

LEWISHAM Open Door for lesbians and bisexual girls and women under 25. Lewisham Young Women's Project, 308 Brownhill Rd, Catford SE18 020 8698 667

MERTON MYNORS (Merton Youth Not of Rigid Sexuality) Noon-6.00pm and Wed 6.30-9.30pm 020 8646 3033

NEWHAM New Dyke for lesbian and bisexual young women under 25, Tues 7-10pm 020 8555 8186

Together for lesbian, gay and bisexual young people 020 8555 8186

SOUTHWARK Outlinks for lesbians, gay men and bisexuals under 26. Tues 5.30-7pm 020 7378 8732

N.R.G. Project for lesbian, gay and bisexual young people aged 16-25. 1 Rushworth Street, London SE1 0RB. Thurs 6-10pm 020 7620 1819. Email nrg@lads.demon.co.uk

TOWER HAMLETS Phase! LGB youth project for info, support, advice and Not the Only Fruit group for young lesbians. 76 St Leonard's St, Bow, London E3. 020 7515 4617. Email youthservice@dial.pipex.com

WALTHAM FOREST SPD for lesbian and bisexual women under 26. PO Box 12045, London E4 9YF. Mon 10am-8pm 0589 422854

WANDSWORTH shOUT! Lesbian, gay & bi youth group. 020 8675 0306.

WESTMINSTER Faces in Focus 102 Harper Road, London SE1 6AQ. 020 7403 2444, fax 020 7207 2982

Nationwide

Lesbian and gay youth groups and helplines ('switchboards'), by town or area

Banbury

Lesbian, gay and bisexual youth group. Cherwell Division Youth Office, The Mill Cottage, Spiceball Park, Banbury OX16 8QE

Bangor

North Wales Lesbian Line. Tues 7-10pm 01284 351 263

Belfast

Cara-Friend. Mon-Wed 7.30-10pm 028 9032 2023

Lesbian Line. Thurs 7.30-10pm 028 9023 8668

Northern Ireland Gay Rights Association. PO Box 44, Belfast BT1 1SH. 028 9664 111. Email: jeffdudgeon@hotmail.com

Bradford

BLAGY Bradford lesbian and gay youth group meets weekly. PO Box 267, Bradford BD1 5XT. 01274 744224

Bridgend

Helpline for gay, lesbian and bi young people. GYL Project, PO Box 29, Bridgend, CF35 6XL. Mon-Fri, 4-8pm 01656 649990

Brighton

Allsorts Youth Project Under 26. 07932 852533. Email allsortsyouth@yahoo.com

Brighton Lesbian and Gay Switchboard and youth project for 16-19. 01273 204050

Bristol

Freedom Youth for young people who are lesbian, gay, bisexual or questioning their sexuality, aged 25 and under, meet weekly. Helpline Mon & Thurs 10am-3pm 0117 955 3355. Email freedomy@dircon.co.uk

Birmingham

The Maypole Group young gay, lesbian and bisexual young people under 21s. PO Box 6722, Birmingham B15 1AB. 0121 359 3864

Bournemouth

Lesbian & Gay Helpline. Mon-Fri 7.30-10.30pm 01202 318822

Cambridge

Kite Club termtime group for lesbian, gay, bi, transgender under-19s. c/o Box Kite Club, Arjuna, 12 Mill Rd, Cambridge CB1 2AD. Email kiteclub@hotmail.com

Cardiff

Cardiff Friend. Helpline 8-10pm Tues-Sat 029 203 40101

Cardiff Triangle for help with housing. 029 2061 9666

GYL Project for young lesbian, gay or bisexual people. PO Box 29, Bridgend CF35 6XL. Mon-Fri 4-8pm 01656 649 990

Chester

Utopia GLB Youth Group. c/o Calypso Youth Information Shop, The Groves, Chester CH1 1SD.
Tues 7-10pm 01244 323330

Chorley

Gay, Lesbian and Bisexual Drop-in, Youth and Community Services, 55 Union Street, Chorley PR7 1EB

Corby

Lesbian Line. 24 hours 01536 393500

Coventry

Godiva Young Gays and Lesbians for lesbians, gay men and bisexuals, meets Coventry and Solihull. c/o The HIV Network, 10 Manor Road, Coventry

Ultimate Karma for Asian gays, lesbians and bisexuals. 0973 865 006 or 0973 523 124

Croydon

Croydon Young Lesbian and Gay Group. Sun 7-10pm 07071 225577

Derby

Lesbian Line, PO Box 140, Derby DE1 1XS. Wed 7-9pm (24-hour answerphone) 01332 341411

Edinburgh

Lesbian Line, PO Box 169, EH1 3UU. Mon & Thur 7.30-10pm 0131 555 0751

Stonewall Youth Project, PO Box 4040, Edinburgh, EH3 9YH. Email Syp@dircon.co.uk

Stonewall Girlz for lesbian and bisexual youth 14-25. 0131 622 2266

Essex

Lesbian, Gay and Bisexual Youth Group, Essex County Youth Service, Thurrock East Locality, Hassenbrook Road, Stanford Le Hope SS17 0NS

Glasgow

Biggles for bisexual, lesbian and gay youth at Phace West on 0141 332 3838

Lesbian & Gay Centre, 11 Dixon St. 0141 221 7203. Website www.gglc.org.uk

Lesbian Health Service 0141 211 8130

Lesbian Line 0141 354 0400

Strathclyde Gay and Lesbian Switchboard 0141 332 8872

Young Lesbian Peer Support Project, Glasgow Women's Library. Lesbian and bisexual women from 14-25 years group 0141 552 8345 or 0141 552 7539

Gloucestershire

Lesbian, Gay and Bisexual Youth Project 01242 226905

Proud Start Friend Project. Lesbian, gay and bisexual youth group for 14-21-year-olds. Mon-Fri 7.30-10pm 01452 306800

Hastings

Hastings and Bexhill District Youth Services for lesbian, gay and bisexual young people. 47 Wellington Square, Hastings TN34 1PT. 01424 430493 or 01424 439284, fax: 01424 430485

Hampshire

BLAGH lesbian, gay and bisexual youth 01420 87339

LGB Youth Group for those questioning their sexuality or wanting to meet other young people 023 9247 2813

Huddersfield

Youth Group for under 25s. PO Box 293 Huddersfield HD1. Tues and Sun 7-9pm 01484 538070

Hull

Lesbian line 01482 214331.

Huntingdon

Freedom Club LGB youth group for 16-23s. 01480 398036. Email lgbfreedom@hotmail.com

Lancashire

One in Ten lesbian, gay and bisexual youth. 0498 924 164 or 01772 621 165

Leeds

Libby and Out for lesbian and bisexual women 15-25. Call Lesbian Line Tues 7.30-9pm on Leeds Gay Switchboard 0113 245 3588

Leicester

Lesbian Gay & Bisexual Centre/ First Out Youth Group 0116 254 7412

Soft Touch Arts/Hyped Project Arts group for young lesbian, gay bisexual youth. 120a Hartopp Road, Leicester LE2 1WF. 0116 270 2706

Liverpool

Liverpool Friend helpline for gay and bisexual women, Tues and Thurs 7-10pm 0151 708 0234

Gyro lesbian, gay and bisexual youth group. 36 Bolton Street, Liverpool L3 5LX. 0151 708 9552

Young Lesbian and Bisexual Women's Group for under-25s 0151 707 2433

Macclesfield

GLYM lesbian, gay, bisexual youth group for 14-25s, Weds 7-10pm at 33 Great King Street, Macclesfield. 01625 501203

Manchester

LGYM Peer support project for young lesbian, gay and bisexual people. PO Box 153, Manchester M60 1LP. 0161 274 4664.

Lesbian and gay group for 14-25s and bisexual group for 14-25s 0161 274 4664

FFLAG Support for young gays and their families. PO Box 153, Manchester M60 1LP. 0161 628 7621

Milton Keynes

Lesbian Gay and Bisexual Youthline for confidential support, and weekly social group for young LGBs. Helpline Wed 7.30-9.30pm 01908 587 677

Newcastle upon Tyne

Tyneside Young Lesbian Project for young women aged 14-25 questioning their sexuality, c/o 13 St James Street, Newcastle upon Tyne NE1 4NF. 0191 261 2277

Newcastle Lesbian Line. Tues 7-10pm 0191 261 2277

Outpost Housing Project. Supported accommodation project for young lesbians and gay men. 13 St James Street, Newcastle upon Tyne NE1 4NF

Norwich

Standout gay youth group, The Matthew Project, Pottergate, Norwich. 01603 763641

Norwich Lesbian Line Tues 7-9pm 01603 625 822

Northampton

Lesbian Line 01604 250887

First Out youth group 01604 628986.

Nottingham

Young Lesbian Group for under-26s. Base 51, 51 Glasshouse St, Nottingham NG1. 0115 952 5040

Youth Support Line group for lesbians and gay men up to 25 in the Mansfield area, call 7-8pm Mon 01623 428459

Oldham

Project for lesbian, gay and bisexual young people in Oldham and Tameside. Education Offices, Old Town Hall, Middleton Road, Chadderton, Oldham OL9 6PP. 0161 911 4258/ 0161 627 2325. E-mail: els.g.beech@oldham.gov.uk

Oxford

Wayout lesbian, gay and bisexual group for under-25s 01865 243389

Penzance

Lesbian Line, PO Box 41, Penzance TR18 2XY. Thurs 8-10pm 01736 753709

Reading

ReachOUT Lesbian, gay & bisexual youth group, PO Box 75, 35-39 London St, Reading RG1 7DU. 0118 958 5010, fax 0118 959 4357, also at The Old Morgue, Burlington Avenue, Slough SL1 2JT. 01753 694225

Rotherham

Lesbian, Gay and Bisexual Youth Group Helpline Tues and Fri evenings 01709 821523

Youth Start, c/o Education Office, Norfolk House, Walker Place, Rotherham S60 1QT. 01709 822564, fax 01709 372056. E-mail:geoff.eagle@rotherham.gov.uk

Runcorn

GLYSS gay & lesbian youth support services in Runcorn, Widnes and Warrington 01925 244 673.

Synergy gay and lesbian youth group in Runcorn. 79-81 Church Street, Runcorn WA7 1LG. Tel/fax 01928 580270

Sheffield

Next Generation Project weekly drop-in run by and for lesbian, gay, & bi young people 0114 270 0298

Gay Girls Group for lesbian and bisexual women, 14-25 PO Box 487, Sheffield S1 2JL. 0114 270 0298

Lesbian and gay youth project, c/o Youth Service, Education Department, Leopold Street, Sheffield S1 1RJ. 0114 273 6605, fax 0114 273 6279. Email d.gault@sheffield.gov.uk

Shrewsbury

Inter-Action, PO Box 189, Shrewsbury. 01743 344179, fax 0118 959 435

Southampton

Breakout Lesbian, Gay and Bisexual Youth Project, Room 6, Northam Centre, Kent Street, Southampton SO14 5SP. 01703 223344

Southend

BLAG young gay and lesbian group 01702 343134

Lesbian and bisexual women 01072 618886

Women's Coming Out Group 01072 344355

Stockport

Young Lesbian/Bisexual Project, PO Box 93, Stockport SK1 3FJ. 0161 477 4096

Stoke-on-Trent

Galaxy Youth for 14-21s. Sat 1-4pm 01782 201177. Email galaxy_youth@hotmail.com

Suffolk

Oasis lesbian and gay youth group, for under-26s 01473 212165

Surrey

Sp@ce lesbian, gay & bi youth group for under-25s 01372 731011

Swansea

Lesbian Gay and Bisexual Switchboard, Thurs 7-9.30pm 01792 480044

Women's Centre for activities for young lesbians. 25 Mansell St, Swansea. 01792 410099

Swindon

Young & Gay Awareness Project for 16-25s 01793 694700

Warrington

GLYSS gay and lesbian youth support services, 49 Wilson Patten St, Warrington WA1 1PG. Tel/fax 01925 633 053

Winchester

Out Youth for 16-25s, c/o Face to Face, 25 City Road, Winchester.. 01962 878300

The House Young Peoples' Project and The Gay Andover Project (GAP), The Drop-In Centre, Winchester Road, Andover SP10 2ER. 01264 332053

York

York Lesbian Line, PO Box 225, York Y01 1AA. Friday 7.30-9pm 01904 646812

USA

Telephone

If you live in the United States, there is a national toll-free number you can phone for advice and support. Phone the Gay/ Lesbian National Hotline at 888-843-4564 or, just check your local phone book under "Gay". There may be a lesbian and gay info and support hotline in your town.

The web

If you have access to the Internet, you will be able to find dozens of sites that will offer you help, support, information and entertainment. Some useful ones are:

www.elight.org

An online community forum for lesbian, gay, bisexual and transgendered youth with personal ads, coming out stories, news and feature articles to read.

www.temenos.net/links/Generations/Youth

This is a very helpful resource list for young people questioning their sexuality.

www.geocities.com/WestHollywood/2680/hotlines.html

The vast WestHollywood site has all sorts of interesting lesbian and gay pages. This one offers information on helplines around the USA, including the National Toll Free number and helpful links.

www.queeramerica.com

This is a fantastic national youth database from OutProud, the National Coalition for Gay, Lesbian, Bisexual and Transgender Youth. There are several different ways to search and by typing in your area code, it will give you a referral list of organisations near your home.

www.lesbian.org

Starting point for dozens of lesbian-related sites and lists

Organisations

Most college and university campuses have a lesbian and gay organisation of some kind, and many of them welcome non-students as members.

For help and advice in coming out to your parents, or for support for them after you're out, contact Parents and Friends of Lesbians and Gays (PFLAG), Box 27605, Washington DC, 20038. Phone (toll-free) 800-432-6459 or (202) 638 4200.

Lesbian Herstory Archives, www.datalounge.net/network/pages/lhall PO Box 1258, New York, NY 10116. (718) 768-DYKE.

National Center for Lesbian Rights, Suite 570, 870 Market Street, San Francisco, CA 94102. (415) 392 6257. Legal advice for lesbians, campaigns on lesbian issues.

Queer America, OutProud!, PO Box 24589, San Jose, CA 95154-4589. National coalition for lesbian, gay, bisexual and transgendered youth.

LYRIC (Lavender Youth Recreation/ Information Center) 127 Collingwood, San Francisco, CA. Toll-free 800-246-7743. Crisis counselling for those under 24 (415) 863-3636.

Hetrick-Martin Institute, 2 Astor, Place, New York, NY (212) 674-2400. Support services for lesbigay youth. Also publishes Your Are Not Alone, resource directory.

Read

Curve, One Haight Street, Suite B, San Francisco, CA 94102. (415) 863-6538. Subscriptions: (818) 760 8983. www.curvemag.com Monthly lesbian glossy includes "Hey, Baby" focus on a young dyke every issue.

Girlfriends, 3415 Cesar Chavez St, Ste. 101, San Francisco, CA 94110. (415) 648-9464. Subscriiptions: 800-GRL-FRND. www.girlfriendmag.com. Monthly lesbian glossy with celebrity interviews, news, reviews. Also publish lesbian erotic magazine, On Our Backs.

Alice, 41 Freitas Ct, Santa Rosa, CA 95407. (707) 526 5965. ecochicks@earthlink.net Bimonthly magazine with news, reviews, edgy, alternative articles "for women on the other side of the looking glass". Lots of lesbian content.

girl 2 girl

From the editors

Working with girls

* Norrina Rashid talks about her experience of working with young women

Almost all my working life I have worked with young women. My openness and honesty have displayed to many young people that like them I am human and I also happen to be a lesbian. This openness has allowed young women confident of their heterosexuality to work through their homophobia. Perhaps more importantly it has given young women struggling with their sexuality a safe place to explore their emotions, deepest fears, hopes and anxieties.

I began my work as a youth worker in 1985. In a small town like Bradford it was not easy for young women, let alone young Asian women, to explore their sexuality. Especially if it was to encompass words such as lesbian or bisexual.

Growing up is difficult enough in its own right. When a young woman is not given permission to express herself or explore her sexuality, it is difficult for her to be happy, confident, content – or to be herself. For young people, to explore their sexuality does not mean they will then become lesbian, gay, bisexual or transgendered. To explore is to look for contentment and happiness whatever the sexuality. They are finding out for themselves rather than assuming the heterosexuality which has been impressed upon them since birth.

For those who are attracted to other girls it's usually a powerful, confusing and difficult time. Perhaps because we know only too well the homophobia which surrounds us. Maybe we have been guilty of laughing at the school 'lezzie'. Maybe we didn't laugh. Maybe we saw the way she was bullied, her pain and isolation. Why would we want to be like her?

I have sat in many rooms with young women and been asked so many questions. Questions which are so painful. Young women asking if they are mentally ill, abnormal or just plain evil. Emotional questioning which breaks your heart. These young women are isolated and scared. So scared that they don't even want to meet other young women 'like them'. So deep is the fear and isolation that to die would be heaven.

But with the help of stepping stones like this book, friends, family, youth groups, supportive adults and workers, the girls begin to blossom. I have watched many lives change from deep fear, pain, depression and isolation to joy, happiness and a thirst for life.

Teachers, youth workers, carers or anyone who wants a current list of reports from local authorities, research, books and resource packs on working with young lesbian, bisexual, gay and transgendered youth should contact: National Youth Agency, Information Team, 17-23 Albion St, Leicester LE1 6GD. Tel 0116 285 3700. Email carolyno@nya.org.uk

Picking up the pieces

*Jane Hoy stresses that colleges and universities need to be safe places

I have worked in adult and continuing education for many years and so I regularly meet prospective students who did not go straight from school to college. One reason for the delay is homophobia. When girls don't feel able to be themselves at home or at school, it affects their schoolwork, their exam results, their ability to make plans for the future – and so their prospects of university. It may only be later, when they are coming to terms with themselves as lesbian or bisexual, that they look at their lives and try to take up those missed opportunities by enrolling for evening classes.

I had seen their problems from the adult end but co-editing this book with Norrina is the first time that I have worked so closely with young people, particularly young lesbian, bisexual and transgendered people. I became a lesbian in my early thirties when I was independent so I don't have much direct experience of what it feels like to be a young woman questioning your sexuality when you are still very dependent on the love and support of your family and friends. But as I listen to the contributors talking about their experiences and read their accounts, I realise that in some ways we have more in common than I first thought.

Debates over definitions of who qualifies as a lesbian continue to rage. Coming to terms with who you are and finding others like yourself is a central theme in the book. Like some of the contributors, I have had my share of comments which served to exclude me, so I find myself identifying with some of the accounts in the book. Other lesbians have told me: "You can't be a lesbian because you don't look like one," or "You can't be one because you haven't been one long enough!"

What I find refreshing about the young women's poems and narratives is that, struggles over internalised homophobia apart, their work reflects a healthy refusal to fit into old boxes. The desire to define their own lives and contributions to a diverse LGBT community is as strong as it has ever been. Their work has made me take a closer look at the way I live my life as a lesbian and some of the beliefs with which I feel a bit too comfortable.

One of the contributors tells us that after watching the film *Stonewall*, she felt so moved at all that lesbians and gays had fought and died for that she decided staying in the closet was not an option. It's far more difficult than it should be for young people to find out more about the history and experiences of the lesbian and gay community. Schools, colleges and unversities could do a lot more to introduce all students to the research and writing of LGBT people.

In the first flush of excitement coming out in the 1980s, and supported by a straight woman colleague, I organised some of the first lesbian studies courses in university adult education. Women of all ages and backgrounds came

161

along, including 'out' lesbians and many who were questioning their sexuality. Meeting other like-minded women in clubs and pubs can be daunting but the classes were a safe space to explore ideas and experiences. This opportunity is now lost. The college where I work is no longer offering lesbian studies and as far as I know there is no publicly funded open access programme in London where lesbians can share experiences and learn about their histories. It's ironic, when the Government is currently funding 'widening participation' projects for marginalised and excluded communities.

In many ways this is a celebratory book. But it's a celebration of a determination to overcome adversity, over the fear and self-hatred generated by homophobia. Over the months Norrina and I put the book together, I have been struck by the honesty of the young women's own accounts in contrast to the hatred, hypocrisy and confusion whipped up by Section 28 of the Local Government Act. As I write this in July 2000, this climate of hate flourishes as we have again lost the vote in the House of Lords to repeal Section 28 of the Local Government Act.

Although no successful prosecutions have ever been made using this piece of reactionary legislation, the possibility remains, effectively distracting attention away from the central question of lesbian and gay rights. Our only hope is that change is possible, as the Scottish Parliament is more enlightened and recently threw it out.

So, despite the increasing number of lesbian and gay characters on TV and film, our young people are bombarded with negative messages and we are all constantly exposed to anti-gay and lesbian prejudice, particularly in the press. In such a climate, the voices of the young women in this book bring messages of hope, courage and humour for us all. So let the last word go to Fiona Johnstone who says: "I love being gay. I love the life I lead because of it and I love the fantastic people I meet because of it."